The Essential Guide to Skiing with Children

Penny Pershall

Illustration: Anthony Aspland Associates, L'Heritage, High Street, St Aubin, Jersey CI

Printed by: Dejavu Colour Ltd, London E10 7PY
Cover Design & Origination:
Power Graphics Ltd, London E10 7PY
Cover Photograph: Courtesy of the Austrian Tourist Board
Back Photograph: Philip Hopkins

British Library Cataloguing in Publication Data
Pershall, Penny

ISBN 0-9520396-0-5

First published in Great Britain in 1992 by:
Panic Publishing
Faragha House
Old Priory
Tile Kiln Lane
Uxbridge
UB9 6LU
Tel: 0895 635 445
Fax: 0895 622 843

Copyright © Penny Pershall, 1992

For Katherine, Sam and Francesca. May you enjoy a lifetime of skiing.

ACKNOWLEDGEMENTS

My grateful thanks are extended to everyone who helped with this book. Firstly to Jane and all the reporters who took time out of their holiday or work to visit crèches and kindergartens. To Tony for his cartoons, skier and doctor Mike Bellamy for his medical advice, Rob for his invaluable time, Roger for his help and support, and to Nicky, without whose help this book would never have been completed.

Contents

Introduction

The thought of the whole family going on a ski holiday seems such a wonderful idea. What an opportunity for the children to learn to ski from an early age. Maybe if they start at three they'll be brilliant, possibly even champions by the time they're in their teens.

They can go to ski school and you can ski all day and meet them after their class or maybe by the end of the week, they'll be able to ski with you. They'll love it, all that snow and Christmas card scenery. Sounds perfect, doesn't it?

What could possibly go wrong?

Read on to find out what can and does go wrong with taking young children skiing and the best ways to avoid the problems. Remember, if they don't enjoy the holiday, neither will you.

Read on, too, to discover how children of all ages can learn to ski more safely.

Finally, when you take young children skiing the two most invaluable things to take with you are patience and a sense of humour.

Happy skiing!

Foreword

A child's first skiing holiday can make or break their love for the sport. It is essential that they enjoy themselves to the full. There's nothing more heart rending than coming back from an excellent day's skiing to find a cold, wet and tearful little face.

The secret of success is to keep them warm, dry and happy. Explain their new, alien surroundings, after all, if the mountains seem big to you, they must be huge to someone under four foot high!

You will find this book an invaluable reference for help, advice and information. Penny Pershall, mother and skier has had years of experience from teaching children to ski in Austria, to running her own chalet specialising in taking young children, and has learned the hard way.

Take advantage of her extensive knowledge and thorough research and, you could be looking forward to many years of happy family skiing ahead of you.

Lord Congleton
President of the Ski Club of Great Britain

About the book

This book is designed to help with every aspect of skiing with children, from how to choose a resort to which foods children should eat to maintain their energy levels and combat the cold.

The resort reports set out to show what each individual resort provides for children of different ages. The six-year-olds and over can always join the regular children's ski school, but facilities for five and under differ dramatically from place to place.

To my knowledge, all the facts given were correct at the time of going to press, but it is impossible to guarantee that changes will not be made before the season begins. For instance, a crèche which states there will be an English-speaking guardian may change its staff before you arrive.

The success of chalet parties has always relied heavily upon the amiability and personalities of the staff and the same goes for châlets and kindergartens with nannies.

Young children have very little sense of fear and need no technique, apart from a snowplough. They have a far better sense of balance than adults.

If common sense is applied when taking children skiing for the first time it will not be long before your entire family can ski together – a very rewarding experience.

The information in this book has been compiled from my experience of teaching skiing, looking after children in ski resorts, running a châlet specialising in taking children and being a mother. I hope that it will help to make your skiing *en famille* more successful and enjoyable.

Shall we take them or not?

There's no hard and fast rule about the right age to take children skiing. Each child is different and only you will know about the capabilities and character of your own child.

But generally children aren't ready to start skiing until they are about five plus. Admittedly some children who live year-round in ski resorts are skiing by two and three, but they *are* different; they are bought up with the snow and within a skiing environment and are put on skis as soon as they can walk. By the same token, there are children not bought up in the mountains who are skiing by three, but they are the exception rather than the rule.

The fun and enjoyment children receive from a morning in the front garden once a year building a snowman while Mum makes them a hot chocolate is not necessarily any indication that they'll love skiing.

Being suddenly left for a day in unfamiliar surroundings and freezing conditions with some instructor shouting at them in a different language is not enjoyable, regardless of what fun Mum insisted it would be.

For this very reason most ski schools do not accept children under five years, but there are alternative facilities provided in most resorts so that you can take the whole family.

Ski Kindergartens
Ski kindergartens offer skiing for two- and three-year-olds upwards who are not ready for the mainstream ski school. Children are introduced to skiing with a variety of games, exercises and fun. In some ski kindergartens immediately the children are bored with skiing or tired they can simply go into a playroom where they can read, paint, play or watch children's videos. Lunch is usually provided and the children are picked up at the end of the day by their parents.

Kindergartens
For younger children and children who do not wish to ski at all, kindergartens are provided which offer supervised play. These nurseries often have rest areas so that the children can have a sleep after lunch. Make sure your child has a named back-pack or bag with a change of clothing and a favourite toy.

Crèche
In some resorts crèche or nursery facilities are available for babies, but certainly not in the majority. Again, make sure that your child has a bag containing nappies, a change of clothing, formula, food, a toy and a blanket.

How to choose your resort

When and if you decide to take the children, choosing a resort to suit the whole family requires different considerations from simply choosing a resort for a week of adult fun – not of course, that a ski holiday with the whole family *can't* be fun...whatever you've heard.

School rules usually restrict most families as to when they can take the children skiing, so you're probably looking at Christmas, half-term or Easter, all of which, unfortunately for you, are usually in the high season category.

FACTS TO CONSIDER WHEN CHOOSING A RESORT
Is there a crèche/kindergarten/ski kindergarten?
Does the resort cater for your children's age and needs? Some resorts don't provide crèches or ski kindergartens, so check first or you could be left holding the baby, as they say.

Is the resort popular with the British?

However pleasant it is to get away from other English-speaking people on holiday, a resort which is popular with the Brits is more likely to have a higher proportion of English children. This not only results in your children being able to make friends more easily, but also means that ski classes become more enjoyable for them and in most cases the ski instructors' English will be more proficient.

How far is the crèche/kindergarten/ski kindergarten/ski school from your hotel, centre of town or a bus stop?

Walking a couple of hundred yards with young children is bad enough at the best of times, so with the added disadvantage of bulky ski clothes and snow boots plus hazards such as fresh snow or ice to overcome, their enthusiasm and endurance are considerably weakened (not unlike our own).

Children should carry their own ski equipment, but if on the odd occasion they should decide against it, you'll have to carry theirs as well as your own, so the closer you are to the slopes or bus stop the easier life will be for all concerned.

Are cars banned in the resort?

By no means essential, but one less hazard to worry about with children. Of course, if cars are not allowed, you have to walk or use public transport.

Are there any other activities available?

The more activities available, the more there is to keep them occupied. The majority of resorts now have indoor swimming pools, and some even have outdoor pools, but these tend to be less suitable for young children. Sleigh-rides, tobogganing, rat-track rides, curling, motorised snow bikes, indoor tennis and squash are just a few activities you might find available.

Transfer time

If you're flying, check the coach transfer time to the resort. Four hours on a coach after a two-hour flight with young children is not recommended as the best way to start a holiday.

If you don't have an alternative, take plenty to entertain them. The majority of tour operators stop for a break if a transfer is over 2½ hours.

Level of resort

Although a white Christmas is every child and skier's dream, the reality is not always so attractive. To guarantee snow, high-altitude resorts with glaciers are a must, but the disadvantages of these resorts for young children is that they can be the cold, (-5 to -15C is not that uncommon in late December/early January). At the other end of the scale, a late Easter will very often leave the lower resorts with little or no snow on their lower slopes.

Which direction do the majority of slopes face?

Although north-facing slopes are much colder in December and January due to the lack of sun on them, they will hold the snow much later in the season for the very same reason.

Is there sufficient skiing for your ability?

Although you may convince yourselves that this holiday will be devoted to the children, if the conditions are good you'll want to ski as well, so make sure there are enough pistes to suit your standard too.

Is there snow-making equipment?

Snow-making equipment can make the difference between skiing and not skiing but it cannot make snow in Caribbean conditions of 24C, so is often of little use at the end of the season. It must, however, be said that it does do a good job if the weather is cold enough.

Choosing accommodation

In most resorts you will have the choice of hotels, self-catering accommodation or chalets, all of which have their advantages and disadvantages.

HOTELS

The wonderful thing about hotels, as we all know, is that someone else does the work. Many hotels also offer health and leisure facilities and there is a lot to be said about relaxing in a whirlpool bath after a hard day's skiing.

Another advantage of hotels is that they are often better situated in proximity to the town centre than self-catering units and chalets, although obviously this is not always the case.

If you are planning to stay in a hotel with young children then check if the hotel offers crèche facilities or can arrange evening babysitting. Many more hotels now offer an evening intercom/listening service. This is fine, but it does restrict you to staying within the confines of the hotel.

Again, many hotels are now realising the requirements of families and are not only providing sufficient high chairs and booster seats, but are also serving early evening meals for children.

The tour operators have really done their homework and will specify in their brochures each hotel's facilities and their suitability for children, but if you're booking independently then ask the hotel what facilities they offer in regard to children.

Package holidays in hotels with facilities for children are more likely to have plenty of other English children.

CHALETS
Once again, the tour operators have become very aware of the demand for family holidays and have geared their programmes accordingly. Some tour operators have selected catered châlets which take only families with young children. In-house qualified nannies are available for most of the week just to look after their young châlet guests. One room or the lounge is converted into a play area during the day with toys, paints, books and games. Most châlets provide a cassette player, a TV and English videos, but it's good idea to take your child's favourite videos with you.

One of the greatest advantages of a châlet with young children is the homely atmosphere. Although they are in new surroundings and their parents will be gone for most of the day, they will very quickly feel at home, and are far less likely to get upset when the parents go skiing knowing they are in familiar surroundings with familiar people. Then if they are thirsty or hungry they can simply ask someone who, with no language barrier, they have quickly got to know and trust.

If the children want a sleep during the day they can either go to their own room or snuggle up on the sofa for a rest.

Although your child will probably demonstrate and cry when you go skiing each day, the chances are that as soon as you're out of earshot they'll be fine, happily playing and chatting with their minder. *You,* on the other hand, will probably feel distraught and guilt-ridden for the rest of the day. Well, don't. If you're *really* concerned that your child won't settle, 'phone the châlet during the morning.

There is a great comfort in leaving your child for the day in an environment they're slightly familiar with and with girls who you both know. It's not at all like leaving them in an unfamiliar crèche full of strangers. But if you have a child who doesn't like being left with child-minders then take someone they know and trust on holiday with you or leave them at home with someone until they're older.

Nannies in chalets are also usually far more flexible than those in resort crèches and will try to cater for your own personal arrangements and child's requirements.

So despite the occasional lack of bathrooms and hot water, châlets are highly recommended for the hols *avec les enfants.*

SELF-CATERING
Self-catering usually turns out to be the most economical way to go skiing, because you basically have to do everything yourself. You have the freedom to eat where and when you please and can choose between a restaurant or cooking in your own apartment. (By the way, don't forget to take a folding high-chair – alternatively, use a child's car seat.)

The self-catering apartments in France are generally very small and an apartment for four usually means two sleep in the living room. Another disadvantage can be the distance between your apartment and where you have to leave your car in purpose-built resorts.

Another problem is that if you want to go out in the evening you will have to get a babysitter to sit in your apartment because there will be no intercom system and no other in-house facilities.

Although economical, self-catering can be inconvenient if you have to start hiring and fetching your own linen and towels. There is the advantage, of course, that in some countries an apartment will provide more space so that the children can play in your living area instead of just a hotel bedroom. You can also give them drinks and snacks whenever you like instead of calling room service.

If you are driving to your resort then try to stock up on groceries at the last major town before you climb into the mountains – preferably in one of the hypermarkets. Otherwise you will find yourself paying resort prices, which are usually well over the top. Why? Because they have a limited season and a captive market and price accordingly. And be warned: take children's favourites such as Ribena, Marmite, Heinz tomato ketchup and HP sauce with you. They are not always available in foreign countries.

If you are staying in self-catering accommodation with babies, do not forget to take a folding cot and linen with you unless you can make prior arrangements to hire them in the resort.

■ Getting off to a good start

Picture: Austrian Tourist Board

The ski school

Does the ski school have a high proportion of English-speaking instructors?

Children will enjoy themselves and benefit a lot more if they have an English-speaking instructor. If, however, your child is in a class with an instructor who does not speak English and is subsequently unhappy, you have every right to go to the ski school about changing classes. Although it is more comforting and educational for a child to have an instructor who *does* speak English, it is true to say that it is not nearly as important as for an adult, who has to have specific techniques explained. Children can learn as much as they need to by watching and copying.

What's the maximum size of a ski school class?

Although the ski schools all claim a maximum number in a ski class (see Resort Reports), in the school holidays large numbers have been reported. Areas with more than one ski school are more likely to maintain smaller classes.

Do the kindergarten/crèche hours coincide with your ski school hours?

You might think it reasonable that they should, but alas, it's not always the case. This may mean that you will either have to start or leave your ski school at inconvenient times.

If your children are beginners, are there sufficient nursery and easy slopes up the mountain as well as in the village?

If they're very young it won't really matter, but even children in ski school enjoy being able to ski higher up the mountain.

Are the nursery slopes south-facing?

Again there are pros and cons. South-facing slopes are favourable in the early part of the season but beware of them later on when the sun can turn them into green meadows.

Do they supervise lunches?

Supervised lunches are a godsend if you want to enjoy a full day's skiing up the mountain. After morning ski school the class teacher takes the children to a restaurant where lunch is served and they are looked after until ski school restarts in the afternoon. If the ski school does not offer this service then it's up to you to ski down and look after your children for this period between classes, which can certainly restrict your geographical skiing limits (not to mention your alcoholic intake).

Do they organise indoor recreation in extreme weather conditions?

Torrential rain, for instance, is a condition unlikely to provoke everlasting enthusiasm for skiing in your child, but many ski schools offer indoor games, videos and other activities in such adverse weather.

■ **Learning is fun at most ski schools**   *Picture: FVV TUX*

The Do's and Don'ts

The Do's

DO MAKE SURE YOUR CHILD WEARS A HELMET TO SKI.

DO make sure that your child is correctly dressed for the conditions, including helmet, hat, gloves and glasses or goggles, whatever the weather.

DO constantly apply sun-block and lip salve even in cold weather.

DO give yourself 15 minutes extra than you usually need for dressing your child, getting the ski equipment, getting to ski school, etc.

DO take your child around the village to familiarise him with his surroundings – ie. where your accommodation is in relation to the ski school

DO always put the name of your child and the name of your accommodation in your child's pocket.

DO make sure your child has all that is necessary for ski school – boots, skis, poles, lift pass, ski school tickets.

DO make sure that all the clothes are fitting comfortably, and especially check that the ski socks or tights lie smoothly against their legs with no creases and that the ski boots are done up correctly.

DO put some tissues, chocolate and enough money for a hot drink in their pocket.

DO ensure that their ski boots are dry from the night before. A wet inner boot is the quickest route to cold feet. If the boot still seems damp use a hairdryer or cloakroom hand dryer to dry it.

DO have ski gloves or mittens joined by a ribbon running through the sleeves of the ski suit and also have a cord on the sunglasses.

DO introduce them to their ski instructor and make sure that not only do they know the teacher's name but also that the teacher knows their name. Also try and find another English-speaking child in the class who they can make friends with.

DO make sure that they can undo and get out of their ski suit to go to the loo. Tie some ribbon on the zips so that they can grip them easily.

DO insist that they go to the loo before leaving for ski school – in fact before you get them into their ski suit.

■ **Do make sure that your children are correctly dressed for the slopes**

The Don'ts

DON'T LET YOUR CHILD SKI WITHOUT A HELMET.

DON'T push your child to ski at too early an age. It's no good putting them off for life for the sake of a year or two.

DON'T attempt to ski with babies and toddlers in a back carrier.

DON'T attempt to take a child between your knees up a drag lift unless you are an advanced skier.

DON'T under estimate how tired a child can become with the combination of altitude, cold and physical exertion.

DON'T leave booking crèches and kindergartens until you get to your resort.

DON'T let your child ski without a hat in cold conditions.

DON'T ever let your child ski without gloves (the same goes for you).

DON'T let your child chew gum or suck on a sweet while skiing; a fall could cause him to swallow the sweet and choke.

DON'T ski with your children on unfamiliar pistes or use lifts on which you might run into trouble and scare them.

DON'T teach your children what you've been taught. Their point of balance is different from adults' and they can get away with leaning back and not bending their legs. As long as they can snowplough, turn and stop, just let them follow you.

Clothing

The correct ski clothing for children is very important, but if you don't want to go to the expense of buying new outfits then look in your local paper for secondhand ski gear or hire clothing just for the holiday. (Contact Ski 3 Up – 081 669 1771)

Remember that natural fibres are better than synthetic ones because they "breath", letting the air circulate.
Wearing several layers of thin clothing rather than fewer, thicker articles is more practical because the air trapped between the layers will keep you warm.

Synthetic fibres can cause you to sweat, and once the sweat becomes cold, there's very little chance of getting warm again.

WHAT YOU WILL NEED

Underclothes
Long- or short-sleeved cotton vests and tights or thermal underwear.

Socks
Preferably knee-length, well-fitting ski, thick or thin socks. It is very important that there are no wrinkles in the socks when they put their boots on as this will create pressure points against their feet or ankles when skiing. Adults take note too. Socks go over the top of tights, not underneath.

Cotton roll-neck shirts
Pure cotton, with or without zip necks.

Sweater
Medium weight pure wool. Thick sweaters tend to be too bulky under ski suits. Sweat shirts are a good alternative in warmer weather.

Ski-suit
There's a choice between a two-piece or an all-in-one ski suit. The two-piece suit consists of an anorak and salopettes (waterproof dungarees) and is very practical and more economical because the anorak can be worn on its own back home. They are also good for children who are spending time in kindergartens as they can easily remove the jacket when they are inside and just play in their salopettes, whereas a one-piece would have to be taken off altogether. The disadvantage is that when you fall snow can ride up your back.

■ **Invest in good sunglasses**   *Picture: Austrian Tourist Board*

The anorak should have a good zip-up collar, zip pockets and elastic cuffs or inner cuffs. Zip on/off sleeves are very practical. Salopettes must have inner ankle cuffs which are worn over the ski boot.

One-piece suits are very comfortable. Make sure the bottom of the leg is wide enough to stretch over a ski boot.

Even babies and non-skiing toddlers will require a snow suit. Gore-tex is the only totally waterproof material available in ski clothing and costs accordingly. You can waterproof ski suits by spraying with Scotch-Guard regularly. It is preferable to have two ski suits, one for skiing and one for playing in the snow.

Gloves
Children and adults must always wear gloves when skiing, even if it's warm. They will protect hands in a fall against snow burns and the metal edges of other people's skis.

Proper leather ski gloves or mittens with linings are ideal, but mittens are warmer. Plastic gloves, although waterproof, are usually very cold. Knitted gloves are suitable only for babies.

Take two pairs and remember to attach a cord or ribbon to the gloves or mittens and run it through the ski jacket to avoid their getting lost.

Hat
About 50% of body heat is lost through the head, so a hat is vital in cold weather. It can be worn under a helmet with no problem; just make sure it's not so big that it keeps falling over the child's eyes or has a pom-pom on it which will make the wearing of the helmet uncomfortable. Wool or lined nylon hats are both popular. In very cold weather a balaclava will keep the face warm. Even in warmer weather ears can get cold so a headband or ear-muffs are advisable.

Helmet
Children's heads are too important and fragile to put at risk. Although few children are seen skiing with a helmet I hope this book will encourage parents to be more aware of the danger of children skiing without proper head protection.

Loose drag lifts and collisions are the two main causes of concussion in children.

■ **Dressed for action and warmth** *Picture: Austrian Tourist Board*

Cebe are now making adjustable helmets which will last one child for several years, but if you decide against buying one, some resort sport shops have them for hire. Alternatively, hire before you go from Ski 3 Up (Tel 081 669 1771).

Goggles
Single-lens anti-fog goggles are adequate. The colour of the lenses is a personal preference.

Sunglasses
Good sunglasses are essential to prevent sore and damaged eyes (see chapter on Health).

Polarized or mirrored glasses are both effective.

Après ski boots
Thick rubber-soled waterproof lined boots are a necessity for the snow. Wellington boots are not suitable.

Equipment

Until children have stopped growing, there is very little point in buying equipment, unless you have a large family and keep passing it down. Hiring is quite satisfactory and fairly economical.

Competition is so fierce in ski resorts these days that rental equipment is usually of a very high standard, so wait until you arrive before renting. If you do rent before you go, then you have to travel with all the equipment and if there is a problem with the equipment while you are away, there is not much you can do.

Children who are old enough to ski should be old enough to carry their own equipment. This will be made easier for young children if you clip the skis together and use the ski poles as a handle, fixing them to the skis by their straps.

■ **Make sure the equipment fits**

Holiday preparations

Once you have made the decision to take the children and chosen a resort, start to talk to them about skiing. Talk about the snow, how cold it can be, why gloves must be worn and kept on, talk about falling down and falling over, and even describe some of the falls you may have had and always laugh about them (even if they were not so funny at the time). Explain that sometimes falls can be a bit of a shock but you have just got to get up, brush the snow off and carry on. Children often cry when they fall due to hurt pride, but the more they expect to fall, the less it will worry them.

Tell them that they will be in a ski school/kindergarten and will have lots of fun with other children and teach them a couple of words of the language that will be spoken, especially *please* and *thank you*. Explain that they will have lunch with their class and that they will be picked up in the afternoon. Leave as little as possible to surprise them with.

If they are unhappy about any of what you tell them, you will have plenty of time to smooth things out before you go.

Four- and five-year-olds can familiarise themselves with the feeling of skis by walking around the home in patinettes (short plastic skis which strap onto an après ski boot). Just keep them away from the stairs.

Patinettes are usually sold in a pack with ski poles and are available at good ski shops. Alternatively, ask a good friend who is going skiing to bring a set back. If children are of an age when they will be going into children's ski school then a few dry ski lessons will be invaluable.

Dress the children in all their ski-wear, including glasses and goggles, a few times before you go on holiday so that they can become familiar with their new outfits.

Travelling with children

Many families with young children opt for travelling by car to avoid a restrictive luggage allowance and the possibility of flight delays. It is also far more convenient to have a car in certain resorts. So despite a good day's travelling time and a possible overnight stay, you have the advantage of the comfort of your own car with just your family and have the flexibility of deciding to stop when and where you want.

Make sure that your child has his or her favourite toy or blanket with them for comfort. This is also far less likely to get lost when travelling by car. A pillow per person and a couple of blankets will also make that en-route nap more comfortable and these items could become life-savers if you are unfortunate to get stuck on a mountain road for the night because of avalanches (see Stranded). Some drinks and snacks are a good idea for in the car, but don't let them drink too much or you'll be making more pit stops than intended. A carton of baby wipes are invaluable for sticky fingers and faces.

Motorway restaurants are usually very well equipped for children, often having children's outdoor play areas or some even have Lego tables within the restaurant. Once the children have eaten they can amuse themselves while you finish your meal. High-chairs and booster seats are always available and most restaurants provide changing facilities.

Make sure that the children are safely strapped in the back of the car with the necessary car seat or booster seat. The AA recommend the Euroseat for long-distance travel for children aged from 8 months to 7 years. Apart from the safety and comfort features, the seat also has a matching table with a plastic top which is ideal for drawing and reading. There are also storage pockets on each side of the seat for pencils and crayons. This seat fits any car with three-point adult seat belts. The AA also rent roof boxes.

The main problem with driving long distances with children is the boredom factor, although toddlers will probably sleep periodically.

Winter sun magnified through windows can become uncomfortably hot so car sun shades are a good idea to protect young children and babies.

CAR SICKNESS

To avoid car sickness:
Take Cinnarazine one hour before travelling (available at good chemists, dosage as on bottle, safe for five years and over). It will last for eight hours and make the children a little sleepy.
Use Phenergan for under fives (dosage as on bottle).
Use acupuncture point bands (the type used to avoid sea-sickness).

To cure car sickness:
Eat ginger in syrup (so take some with you).

Sitting in the front seat is also a good cure, but without proper children's safety belts (ie a baby harness) is illegal in most European countries (see Belting Up – Children and the law).

ACTIVITIES

Colouring and activity books.
Coloured pencils (sellotaping or tying each crayon to a separate 12-in piece of string and tying them all together will prevent losing them down the back of car seats or on the floor.
Picture books.
Personal stereos and cassettes of children's stories or perhaps langauage tapes.

GAMES TO PLAY
For young children
I spy, using colours for younger children.
First person to spot a church, red car, cow, mountain, etc.
The "Yes, No" game. (In which you must not use those words.)
I went to the market and bought an apple (–this game can last a long time if you insist on going through the alphabet).
One person makes up one sentence and everyone has to add to it.
Reading to them – if it doesn't make *you* car sick.
Word association games.
Opposites.
Glove puppets for the *really* entertaining mum.
Jig-saws and games with small pieces will inevitably end up on the floor and down the side of the seat, so try to avoid them.

For older children and adults
Junior Trivial Pursuit – just take the cards if you don't want to buy a travelling pack.
The Mr and Mrs game. (Everyone has to think up names such as Mr and Mrs Wall Carpet and their son Walter Wall Carpet, or Mr and Mrs Saur and their daughter Dina Saur.)
The "Yes, No" game.
Animal, vegetable or mineral.
20 Questions (choose to be a famous fictitious or non-fictitious person, place or object).

THE CAR – WHAT TO TAKE

A red triangle – compulsory in Europe.

A first-aid kit – compulsory in Switzerland.

Snow-chains – Buy or hire them. **Do not wait until your half way up an alp to learn how to put them on** – make sure you have had a dry-run at home. And don't think that you can do without them if you're driving in the mountains. Some mountain roads and resorts in Europe have compulsory snow-chain laws. An illuminated snow-chain sign at the beginning of an ascent (or in the village) must be obeyed to avoid an accident and a heavy fine. Snow-traction clamps are not suitable because they are only for emergencies.

De-icer – Ice on the windscreen can be quickly and easily removed with the help of an aerosol de-icer and ice-scraper.

Scraper – A plastic scraper is invaluable for clearing ice and frost from the windows. Should you not have one then a credit card will do the job.

Shovel – If your car's been parked outside in a resort after a heavy snowfall you may well be digging it out.

Torch – Should you have to fit chains at night, a little light on the matter will be a great help. Check the batteries before you leave home.

Windscreen washers – Fill up the washer reservoirs before you leave and top up with special additives to minimise smear and stop freezing (ask at your local garage). Take spare window washer fluid with you.

Lock de-icer – Invaluable if you want to get into your car when the lock is frozen. Alternatively, heat the key with a match or cigarette lighter.

Gloves and anorak – An old pair of gloves and an anorak are recommended for putting on the chains, so your new ski gloves and ski jacket will still match for the right reasons.

MOUNTAIN DRIVING

However good and safe a driver you are, driving on snow, ice and slush require certain skills and care so do try to remember the following points:

Going up

If you are climbing in the snow without chains maintain a very steady speed and do not stop. If you do stop you're more than likely going to get stuck. Choose a low gear before you start your ascent to avoid changing gear; removing your foot from the accelerator can have the same effect as braking.

Around the resort – taking it easy
Soft, new crunchy snow is quite easy for tyres to grip but hard-packed snow and ice call for attention. Remember in these conditions that steering and braking should both be done very gently. **Never steer and brake at the same time. Leave plenty of distance between you and the car in front.**
Braking involves a feather-light touch and a gentle pumping action lessens the risk of the brakes locking. The constant flashing of your brake lights also warns the car behind you.
Don't think that changing to a lower gear is the best way to slow down, the action of letting the clutch out can cause the car to slide. **Just drive slowly in a low gear and give yourself plenty of room.** If you should brake and start to skid, release the brakes immediately, then re-apply them quickly but extremely gently. Preferably, try not to get into this predicament.

Going down
It is far more dangerous going down the mountain, so again take care and drive slowly in a low gear. You should be completely in control of your car at all times and know that you can stop at any given moment without the risk of skidding.

It is a fallacy that tyres should be deflated a few pounds to gain better traction. Stick to the manufacturer's recommendations.

STRANDED
This is a possible but unlikely situation. If, however, you are unfortunate enough to get stranded remember the following points:
It is most important to keep warm, so put on your ski clothes and cover yourselves with blankets.
Try to stay awake, although if the children are warmly dressed

let them sleep.
Huddle together for extra warmth.
If there are other people in the same predicament then you are
better all to get into one car.
Only run the car engine for heat if the exhaust is clear of snow.
Occasionally open a window slightly for some fresh air.
A hot drink, sweets and chocolate all help to create body heat.

BELTING UP – CHILDREN AND THE LAW

France – It is compulsory for all children to wear safety belts
and children under ten must not travel in the front if back
seats are available. Babies must be in special seats which are
anchored and the baby must be strapped in to the seat.

Switzerland – It is illegal for children under the age of 12 to
travel in the front of a vehicle unless there is a suitable
restraint system or there are no rear seats.
Children over 12 in the front seat must wear a seat belt.

Austria – It is illegal for children under the age of 12 to travel
in the front seat unless they are wearing special children's
safety belts or are in a special children's seat.

Italy – It is illegal for children under the age of four to travel
as a front seat passenger without a child restraint system.
Children between four and 12 are allowed in a front seat only
with a special restraint system.

Spain – It is illegal for children under the age of 12 to travel
in a vehicle as a front seat passenger unless they are wearing
special children's safety belts or occupy a special children's
seat.

The Automobile Association - tel: 0256 20123
Royal Automobile Club - tel: 0800 181344
Europ Assistance - tel: 081 680 1234

Flying

The advantage of flying is speed. Although unfortunately due to delays, this is not *always* the case. The main disadvantage of flying with young children is not only the distance you have to travel within the airport, but getting on and off buses, escalators and planes bustling with hundreds of other travellers. Some airlines (who seemingly have no idea how heavy a toddler can be) will not allow you take a pushchair all the way to the plane, so you are left struggling with a child plus your hand luggage plus your duty frees. And this is meant to be a holiday?

If a child can walk the required distances without being carried or asking to be carried, flying can be a quick and comfortable way to start the holiday.

Always reserve your seats when you make the flight booking to ensure that all the family sit together. Don't leave it until you check-in.

POINTS WORTH NOTING AND QUESTIONS TO ASK
British Airways will allow you to take a child's car seat on board. All makes with the British Certificate of Safety Standards. As a seat space will be taken, you'll have to buy a children's priced ticket.

Can you book an electric buggy to take you and your family and luggage to check-in and to the aircraft? Although usually reserved for the sick and elderly, many airlines have said they can be pre-booked.

Check if you can take a pushchair right up to boarding the aircraft. Also check if it can be stowed in the cabin so you can have it when you disembark. (This usually depends on how full the aircraft is.)
Find out if the airline embarks and disembarks families with

young children first. If the answer is no, then board last. It's easier to get yourselves sorted out when everyone else is seated. There's also less time before take-off.

If you have to travel with a two-year-old on your lap and the aircraft is not full, ask the air hostess if she could move the person next to you to allow you extra space. By all means back up your request by mentioning that your child usually screams/vomits/kicks/throws food when travelling.

Do they serve children's food? Many airlines do but who ever knew? Kiddies' favourites can be served but must be ordered in advance.

Do they provide cots? Usually only for long haul but again most airlines carry a limited number. Book in advance.

Are there changing tables aboard? Some aircraft have changing tables which simply fold down in the toilet. Although you're unlikely to change your flight if they don't, it's good to know what to expect.

If you are travelling with a large family of youngsters can you receive extra assistance? Assistance if requested well in advance is available from check-in to the gate. Finally, does the airline carry emergency baby packs of nappies, formula, food and wipes ?

Train

Travelling by train through snow-covered passes is enchanting not to say romantic – but not very suitable for young children. The availability of seating and trolleys is worse at railway stations than airports, so although most children love travelling by train, it is not recommended for young families. But should you choose this method of transport take plenty to amuse the children.

Health

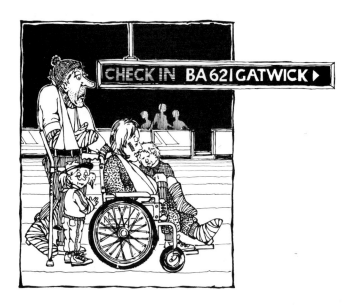

CHECK IN   BA 621 GATWICK ▶

We all accept the risks of skiing and are prepared for the possibility of a few bumps and bruises, but give a thought to the mountains. Majestic and beautiful as they are, like any environment they are subject to rapid condition changes. The height, sun and cold all bring problems of their own. But don't be put off, most of the following ailments can be avoided by taking sensible precautions.

Fatigue
Although not an illness as such, the combination of altitude, cold and physical exertion all contribute to children tiring quicker than normal. Fantastic, you're probably thinking, what's the problem? Well none, but they must have a good carbohydrate intake at lunchtime to keep their energy levels up to combat the cold and exercise. A good breakfast and mid-morning and afternoon warm drinks will also help.

Fortunately for parents who want an easy time on holiday, the foods that are high in carbohydrate and easily obtainable in restaurants also happen to be most children's favourites. Pasta, pizza and chips are all good fodder for our skiing offspring. They won't believe it, and naturally if we don't tell them it's good for them, they'll just think we're the greatest parents in the world (as if it were ever in question).

Altitude sickness

From about 2,500m upwards children and adults can suffer from altitude sickness. Although not such a problem in Europe, it is quite common in American ski resorts, where the accommodation tends to be at a higher level.

The symptoms can include evening tiredness, restless sleep, morning frontal headaches, a tight chest and vomiting, all of which may last up to three days but usually subside of their own accord. Complete rest is advisable during this time.

Snow blindness

I cannot stress enough how important it is for children, babies and adults to have good sunglasses, which must be worn on sunny *and* cloudy days, and replaced by goggles when it is snowing.

Snow reflects 80% of the UV light and there is just as much UV light on a cloudy day as on a sunny day.

Over-exposure to UV light will result in sore eyes and even snow-blindness, which causes the eyes to become red with painful 'sandy' itching. It can even lead to loss of sight for up to two days in more severe cases. On a long-term basis snow blindness can cause corneal ulcers. If at the end of a day's skiing you or your children complain of sore eyes the best treatment is rest. If , however, the soreness continues consult a doctor.

Frostbite

Toes, fingers, ears and noses are the most at risk in very low temperatures, especially if there is also a wind chill factor. Again, this is more frequent in America, where, fortunately, the lift attendants are very quick to send you in if they see any signs of frostbite or hypothermia.

Bad circulation and over-exposure to cold conditions all contribute to this condition.

Make sure children are wrapped up warm and have proper ski gloves or mittens, hats or even balaclavas in cold weather. **In extremely cold temperatures keep them in.**

About 50% of the body heat is lost through the head so make sure they always wear a hat. Children in particular lose body heat rapidly in cold conditions and babies will lose heat even more quickly so keep them well wrapped up if they are outside.

If children complain about cold fingers then get them to swing their arms over and over in large circles to improve circulation.

Hypothermia
Little body fat, inadequate clothing, sensitivity to cold, exhausting exercise and lengthy exposure to sub-zero conditions all contribute towards hypothermia. Babies and young children born at sea level do not tolerate the cold as well as children born at high altitude, and because children, especially babies, lose body heat rapidly in cold conditions it is imperative that they are warmly dressed. If they do suffer from exposure warm them slowly but not directly in front of a fire.

But use common sense. If the temperature is well below zero or it's slightly below with a wind chill factor, keep them indoors. However cold it is in the town, it's going to be colder on the slopes. And don't be misled by the sun. In January a beautiful sunny day will be colder than a cloudy day, because the warm air is not trapped under the clouds.

Sunburn
Sunburn can and should be avoided at all costs. There really is no excuse for sunburn with the range of protective products available.

Whatever the conditions, apply a total sun-block to faces and later in the season to the ears and neck as well. Also apply lip protector and put one in their pocket so they can re-apply it themselves. If you will not be seeing your child at lunchtime and therefore are unable to re-apply the sun-block, ask the ski instructor to do it.

Other altitude-related illnesses
Tummy upsets.
Weight loss.
Sleep disturbance (and not the one caused by the rest of the chalet guests returning from the local nightclub).
Problems for diabetics – see your doctor for advice before you go, but sometimes less insulin is needed.

The travelling medicine cupboard
It is wise to take a few emergency medicines with you to prevent your having to buy them in a resort.

Dioralyte – for rehydration after diarrhoea or tummy upsets.
Calpol – As if any mother would travel without it!
Aqueous cream BP – a good moisturiser.
Imodium syrup – to stop diarrhoea.
Zovirax – If they suffer from cold sores.
After-sun soother – Just to cool the skin if you've not kept the sun block up sufficiently.

Babies

There is absolutely no reason why you should not take babies to the mountains as long as they are in good health. Up to six months is, in fact, a particularly easy time to take them, as they sleep the majority of the time and just require exactly what they would require if they were at home. They are not yet crawling so are not constantly on the move.

Travelling
If you are driving to the resort strap baby into a rear-facing car seat which also acts as a carrycot. Normal carrycots, even with safety straps, are not suitable for cars because the baby is not strapped in.

To warm baby's bottle en-route, most garages and motorway restaurants have micro-waves. Alternatively, invest in a travel bottle warmer by Childcare Products Ltd, which does not require batteries or mains.

Flying with babies should not cause any problems, but let them drink on take-off and landing to avoid any build up of pressure in their ears.

What to take
Enough formula for the trip plus 2 extra bottles for delays and emergencies. Water or juice for baby to drink, prepared meals if on solids, spoons, bibs, nappies, wet wipes, favourite toy, Calpol, cloths for your shoulder, nappy cream, baby lotion, talcum powder, a change of clothing for baby and a change of top for you.

Clothing
A padded snowsuit – some even come with poppers or zips for changing nappies.
A warm hat and gloves.
Sunglasses or baby goggles – available at good sports shops (see chapter on Health).

In the resort
Don't bother to take a pushchair because they are not much use in the snow. Carry small babies in a sling or back carrier and hire a toboggan with a basket seat attached for babies over six months.

Do not attempt to ski with your baby, however skilled you are; someone else could easily run into you.

The altitude should not cause any undue problems. Babies ears can equalise pressure easier than an adult because the eustachian tubes in their ears are wide open. A problem may arise if the baby has a cold and the tubes become blocked, because air expands at low pressure and will cause pain in the ears. A decongestant, such as Sudafed, should be administered (dosage as on bottle) in such cases.

Always apply sun block protection cream at altitude whatever the weather and put ski sunglasses or goggles on your baby if you are outside.

Do pre-book crèches and kindergartens.

What holiday companies offer families

A t last the tour operators seem to have woken up to the fact that skiers are parents too and sometimes they'd like to take their children skiing and have a little more offered than a small discount and a cot in an undersized hotel room.

Not surprisingly some skiers who did have families realised this niche in the market many years ago and some very good small companies started very successfully, specialising in taking families with young children.

So now there's an ever increasing choice of facilities available. Many major operators offer chalets with qualified nannies in attendance or hotels with in-house crèches. Some operators have even started their own children's clubs in selected resorts, so as far as parents are concerned things are really looking up. Listed below is a concise guide to exactly what the ski companies do offer families with young children.

Only bonded tour operators have been included.

Bladon Lines – *Major operator. Chalets, hotels and self-catering.*
Offer own private crèche in Chalet Hotel Lo Terrachu, Tignes, France. Crèche open for children nine months to six years, Monday to Saturday from 8.30am and 5pm. Qualified English nannies. Price: £85 per week includes lunch and high tea. Cots can generally be pre-booked and paid for before departure. Good discounts for children, granny or nanny coming to look after the them. No restrictions on other chalets if whole chalet is booked. Bladon Lines have chosen hotels that are 'children friendly' and will pre-book nurseries and kindergartens. Brochure from local travel agent. Tel: 081 785 2200.

Crystal – *Major operator specialising in families.*
Have extended their family programme to include two specific chalets in Les Coches, La Plagne (all season) and two in Meribel just for the school holidays. All the chalets have at least one in-house trained nanny and a designated crèche area with plenty of toys and games. The Crystal Nanny Service includes supervision of children from six months to five years, 9.30am to 4.30pm five days a week. Lunch, snacks, drinks, high tea. Organised outside play. One free night's babysitting; extra evening babysitting at £4.95 per hour. Free use of travel cots and high-chairs in chalet. Will also meet older children from ski school. All children welcomed with the Pepi Penguin Club Welcome pack. Price: five full days £75; five half-days £44; £3 per day for lunch or £13.95 per five days.
Families with children under 12 years may book some selected chalets without occupying the whole chalet in school hols only. Brochure also highlights their Family Choice resorts. Good children's discounts.
Brochure from local travel agent. Tel: 081 399 5144.

Club Med – *Have long been established as family specialists.*
Majority of their "villages" cater for children.
Baby Club – four months to one year, open 8.30am to 6pm, six days a week, lunch.
P'tit Club – from two years, open 8.30am to 9.30pm, six days a week (non-skiing kindergarten). Inside and outside play, lunch.
Mini Club – from four years (six at Tignes) open 8.30am to 9.30pm, open every day, ski lessons and indoor activities, lunch.
Kid's Club – eight to 11 years (depending on village) open 9am to 9.30pm. Lunch and supper with parents. Kid's Club is a meeting place where children can choose their own activities and skiing.
Brochure from local travel agent. Tel: 071 581 116.

Ski Enterprise – *Major operator.*
Have carefully selected resorts suitable for families with
children and are well marked in their brochure. Good children's
discounts of up to 50%.
Brochure from local travel agent. Tel: 071 221 0088.

Inghams – *Major operator in 77 resorts across eight countries.*
Specialises in hotels and offers many with kindergartens. Also
self-catering. Good children's discounts.
Brochure from local travel agent. Tel: 081 789 3331

Le Ski – *Small quality chalet operator in Courcheval and Val
d'Isere.*
Very happy to take children. Cots and highchairs available free
of charge. All chalets well located. Free guiding service open to
children who can ski. Will arrange babysitters.
Brochure from 2 Holly Terrace, Huddersfield HD1 6JW. Tel:
0484 548996.

Made to Measure Family Skiing- *Holiday solutions.*
You tell them your requirements and they'll come up with a
solution. New this winter is their colour brochure Family Skiing
which has 18 resorts with information on hotels with
kindergartens and facilities for babies and children. Brochure
from 43 East Street, Chichester, West Sussex PO19 1HX . Tel
0243 533333.

Mark Warner – *Club hotel and Chalet holidays.*
Offer in-house crèches in three Clubhotels in Verbier, Val
d'Isere and Courmayer, for children six months to six years. The
nursery is open from 9am to 5pm, seven days a week, staffed by
qualified English nannies. Childminding is available for
children up to 12 years old. They will deliver and collect
children from ski school, give them lunch and tea. Children not
skiing in the pm will be supervised. Free evening babysitting
listening service from 7.30pm to 11pm. Extra babysitting at £3
per hour can be arranged.   Price: Crèche cost £100 per week
and childminding £75 per week, which includes all meals.
Brochure from local travel agent. Tel: 071 938 3861

■ **Do the tour operators offer the right facilities for children?**

Meriski – *Small quality chalet operator in Meribel.*
Nanny service provided in selected chalets on specific weeks.
Qualified nanny. Plenty of toys, free use of cots and clip on high
chairs. Will transport children to ski schools etc. Brochure from
Fovant Mews, 12a Noyna Road, London SW17 7PH. Tel: 081
682 3883.

Neilsons – *Major operator.*
Have labelled resorts and accommodation with their "Great for families" logo to help you to choose. Good children's discounts. Families with children under 16 must book entire chalet. Brochure from local travel agent. Tel: 0532-394555

Pistes Artistes - *Quality chalet service..*
Offers two chalets in Champery, Switzerland for families equipped with cots, highchairs etc. Nanny service available eight hours a day, seven days a week. Evening babysitting can be arranged. Chalets only three minute walk from ski school. Brochure from Chalet Pampanilla, 1874 Champery, Switzerland. Tel 010 41 25 791520.

Powder Byrne – *Comprehensive service for children*
Nanny service for under fours between 9am to 4.30pm at £95 per child for five days (Weds off). This service is flexible to suit clients. Exclusive use of nanny for £300 per week (up to max. of four children for six days and two nights babysitting). Special arrangements for Christmas week in Grindelwald and Flims for younger children. Powder Byrne Junior Club for five to 11 year olds. Starts Sundays, 9am to 4pm. Children are collected and delivered in a "kid's only" minibus. Club operates in association with Swiss Ski School. Supervised lunch. Brochure from 50 Lombard Road, London SW11 3SU. Tel: 071 223 0601

Simply Ski - *Small family run business.*
Operate Snow-Drop nursery in Chalet Broche, Montchavin, La Plagne, France. Takes from six months to six years, 8.30am - 5pm six days a week (exc. Saturday).
Children in ski school can be delivered, collected and supervised until 5pm. High tea served at 6pm.
All day crèche: £84 per child per week
Half-day supervision: £54 per child per week.
Early booking advised due to limited places. Brochure from 8 Chiswick Terrace, Acton Lane, London W45LY. Tel: 081 742 2541

Ski Esprit - *Established operator specialising in family skiing holidays in France and Switzerland.*
No need to take over a whole chalet to take children, Accommodation in catered chalets. In-chalet well stocked creches for children over 4 months are run by qualified English nannies in all resorts. Strictly adhere to ratio of one nanny to five infants and one nanny to six children(two years and over). Crèches run from 8.30am to 5pm, five days a week, but seven days a week in Morzine and Les Coches. Lunch is provided. Cots and highchairs provided free. Snow Clubs: Action-packed afternoon for four to eight year olds. Ski school pick-up and lunch for all-day skiers. Early suppers. Selection of videos in their larger chalets, cassette players in all. Free evening babysitting two nights a week until 1am in every chalet. Additional babysitting can be arranged. Will arrange birthday parties. Large children's discounts of up to 50%. See brochure for crèche and lunch prices. Brochure from your local travel agent. Tel: 0252 616789.

Ski Famille - *Small chalet company specialising in families with young children in Les Gets.*
Well equipped in-house creche, with free nanny-service four days a week from 9.15am to 4.30am. Extra days available at £15 per child per day. Lunch available for £2.50 per day. Early suppers then children's video in the nursery while parents enjoy a quiet pre-dinner drink. Babysitting available. Chalet has baby bottles, sterilisers, nappies, cots, baby baths, changing tables and highchairs, most of which are free. Games, videos and books for older children.
Good discounts and children not expected to share with parents. Brochure from Unit 9 Chesterton Mill, French's Road, Cambridge CB4 3NP. Tel 0223 63777/66220.

Ski Hillwood - *Specialises in taking children .*
Operates crèche in Hopfgarten and Neustift, Austria, for children six weeks to four years. Open to non Ski Hillwood guests. Qualified staff ratio of 1:4. Very well equipped crèche. Separate area with cots. Children taken out for play, weather permitting. Open Sunday to Friday 9.15am to 4.30pm. £95per week.

Owl club (Hopfgarten only): Introduces children from four to six years to skiing, with play and games. Staff ratio of 1:6. Also indoor games. Home-made lunches and snacks. £95 per week includes ski equipment. Families who book receive a Baby Information Pack. Evening babysitting available most nights by Ski Hillwood's patrol service at 50AS. Accommodation in hotels and self-catering. Free Mothercare cots and highchairs. Children's early suppers. 2 Field End Road, Eastcote, Middlsx HA5 2QL. Tel: 081 866 9993.

Ski Peak - *Chalets and hotels in Vaujany, France.* (Linked to Alp d'Huez). Families welcome and chalets are equipped with cots, highchairs, toys and games. Early suppers for children. Nanny Care Service for chalet and hotel guests for all departure dates in January and April. Available five days a week, 9.30am to 4.30pm for children under four years of age. Cost £75 per week. Vaujany has a ski kindergarten and day nursery. Brochure from Hangerfield, Witley, Surrey GU8 5PR. Tel: 0428 682272.

Ski Scott-Dunn - *Small quality chalet operator with specific chalets for families.*
Operating in Zermatt, Switzerland, Courcheval 1850, France and Champery, Switzerland. In-house nannies work 8.30am to 5pm, six days a week. Plenty of toys, games and videos in chalet. Deliver and collect children from ski school if required. Cost of nanny service per week £140. Will arrange babysitters for evenings at a rate of £4 per hour. Good children and nanny discounts. Brochure from Fovant Mewa, 21a Noyna Road, London SW 17 7PH. Tel: 081 767 0202.

Ski-Tal - *Hotels and catered chalets. for families.*
Operates specific chalets for taking families with young children in France, Austria, Switzerland and Canada.. Facilities differ from chalet to chalet but full-child minding service, 'safe play' areas, baby listening devices, ski school deliver and collect service, free babysitting. Brochure from 2 Criterion Buildings, Wintersbridge, Portsmouth Road, Thames Ditton, Surrey, KT7 0SS. Tel 081 398 9861/8413.

■ **Choose a resort with plenty of activities**   *Picture: Alpach, Austria*
Austrian Tourist Board

Ski Thomson - *Major operators, accommodation in hotels,*
apartments and chalets.
This season have introduced a Family Choice programme, with
pre bookable ski and/or kindergarten/creche, good off the
slopes activities and baby sitting in most resorts. Family choice
accommodation has cots and highchairs for hire, early evening
menus and baby alarms at selected hotels.
Ski Thomson's Peter the Polar Bear Club offers five day
supervision for three to eight year olds from 9am until 4.30pm.
Supervised lunches (at extra cost), well-stocked playroom,

special children's excursions (at small extra charge), early evening stories and child patrolling service from 8pm until midnight two nights a week. This club is available at Val Thorens, France; St Johann, Austria; Risoul, France. Special children's reductions. Brochure from local travel agent. Tel: 081 200 8733.

Ski Total - *Chalet operator.*
If you take a whole chalet, children are accepted on all dates. Two chalets accept families at any time, otherwise the decision is at the management's discretion. Cots and highchairs available at small cost. Early suppers. Will provide transport to skiing/ kindergartens. No nannies of their own but will certainly try and arrange babysitters. Children's discounts. Tel: 081 948 6922.

Snowtime - *Established chalet and hotel operator in Meribel, France.*
Run own crèche on the ground floor of Chalet Le Tronchet. Qualified nannies look after babies of all ages in the well equipped crèche and combine play with a learning programme. Open Sun to Fri, 9am to 5pm. Children can be picked up in the Snowtime minibus from your accommodation and taken to the crèche. Price: Half day without lunch - 150FF, full day with lunch 250FF. Early suppers. Cots and highchairs available. Under 16s accommodated free if sharing room with parents. Baby intercom system in hotels, parent holds the mobile receiver. Evening babysitting can be arranged. Tel: 071 433 3336.

Supertravel - *Quality chalet specialist.*
Have specific chalets for taking families with cots, highchairs. Nannies will work as required and can arrange evening babysitting. Tel: 071 962 9931.

Swiss Chalet Co - *Operates three chalets with nannies.*
Operates in Alpes des Chaux, above Villars, Switzerland. Offers a free child-minding service for children under five years by qualified nanny, five days a week 9.30am to 4.30pm.

Additional babysitting can be arranged. Cots, highchairs etc. available.
Brochure from 8 Deanwood House, Stockcross Newbury, Berkshire RG16 8JP. Tel: 0635 44684.

Swiss Travel Service- *Swiss hotel operator.*
At least a 50% reductiion for children between 2 and 11years.
£95 specials for children between 2 and 5 years inclusive of flight and half-board when sharing with two adults.
Use hotels with kindergarten facilities in Saas Fee, Engleberg, Zermatt and Grachen. Brochure from Bridge House, Ware, Herts SG12 9DE Tel: 0920 463971.

The Ski Company - *Operating solely in La Clusaz, France.*
Offer Family Week, from the 14th February for half-term. All chalets are reserved for families. Organsied children's ski lessons for 8 years and over (younger go to the ESF), apres ski activities arranged all week including fancy dress. If conditions permit a ski race will be held on the final day. Brochure from 13 Squires Close, Bishop's Park, Bishop's Stortford, Hertfordshire, CM23 4DB. Tel: 0279 653 746.

The Ski Club of Great Britain

The Ski Club of Great Britain is the largest ski club for recreational skiers in the world, with a rapidly growing membership.

For almost 90 years the Club has been working to ensure that its members get the best from their skiing.
The advantages of membership include a wide choice of skiing holidays for every standard accompanied by a party leader and the Ski survey colour magazine five times a year, which provides up-to-date information on travel, resorts, snow conditions and equipment. Children over six years are welcome on the specialised family holidays. The Ski Club will ski with and look after your children while you ski and look after yourself.

The SCGB is probably best known for the experience and quality of its ski reps, who are stationed in 35 major resorts in Europe and the USA. The reps are on hand to help you get the very best out of your holiday with helpful advice on where to ski, where to eat and anything else you may want to know.
Your membership entitles you to over 700 discounts on travel, clothing and equipment hire, holidays, medical treatment and dry ski slopes in the UK and abroad.

The lively clubhouse at Eaton Square provides bar and restaurant facilities plus a calender of regular events and is available for private functions.

For aspiring racers the Club annually holds the Verbier Challenge Cup, a giant slalom race open to all standards and ages, and The British Schoolgirls' Invitation Race, which is a complete accompanied package organised for the weekend from Heathrow. The Club also holds a Junior Racing Clinic for one week in April.

For further information and membership details contact: The SCGB, 118 Eaton Square, London SW1. Tel: 071 245 1033.

Insurance

Although insurance may not be one of the most enjoyable aspects of a ski holiday, it is without doubt one of the most essential.

Most tour operators offer an insurance package which will cover you sufficiently for medical expenses, third-party, personal accident, delays, cancellations, and luggage loss or theft. It is usually a condition of booking that you have a ski insurance policy, whether it's the tour operators or your own.

As soon as you put down the deposit on your holiday, take out insurance. So if you do have to cancel, which is quite possible with children, due to some illness, you will be compensated for the loss of your deposit.

Several companies specialise in winter sports insurance and offer special rates. Infants under two years are usually free if travelling with an insured parent and there are reductions for children from two years to 16, provided they are travelling with an insured adult. Family rates usually apply to two adults and any number of dependant children under 16 years of age travelling together.

Contact your own insurance company for further information and do not even consider a ski holiday without adequate cover.

Winter Sports Insurance specialists are:
Douglas Cox Tyrie – tel: 801 534 9595
Fogg Travel- tel: 0623 631331
Matthew Gerard – tel: 0483 715302
Skisafe – tel: 0268 590658
West Mercia – tel: 0902 892661

Guide to the Resort Report

The Resort Report is not a guide describing what each resort is like, but a comprehensive report to what different resorts provide for children.

The General ski information is self-explanatory.
Lift passes are current for the 92/93 season and are generally quoted for high season.

Where there is more than one ski school in a resort, the main or most suitable ski school has been described. Generally, all ski schools keep to approximately the same times and prices.

Although ski schools have given a percentage of ski instructors that speak English, it is impossible to say just *how* much English they know.

If you will be putting your child in a crèche, telephone before you leave for your holiday to see if a health certificate is necessary, most were unsure when we spoke to them. Crèches will not accept children who are ill.

Take proof of the children's age ie. a passport, when you go to buy the lift passes. They may wish to check that your child qualifies for a reduction.

In the majority of resorts a list of babysitters is available at the Tourist office, very often with a list of what languages the girls can speak and what hours they are available. Although the Tourist offices do not ask for references from the girls before they are added to the list, they say they have never had a problem.

Only tour operators that offer a specific service for children are listed in the resort report.

While absolutely every effort has been made to bring you accurate reports from each resort, I cannot guarantee that times, days, facilities and even locations won't be changed after publication.

If on your travels you are extremely pleased with a resort not mentioned or unhappy with resorts that are mentioned I would be very pleased to hear from you (address your report to Panic Publishing, Faragha House, Tile Kiln Lane, Uxbridge UB9 6LU). After all, the aim of the book is quite simply to help and advise parents with children, so the more information we can compile, the more knowledge we can impart.

But please note that the success of your child's stay at a crèche or kindergarten will depend very much on the staff, who usually change every year, which is why I have not made any specific recommendations.

The tour companies listed are not necessarily the only operators who go to the resorts in the 'Resort Report', but they are all included in the chapter 'What holiday companies offer families'.

Once you have decided on a resort, whether you're going with a tour operator or not, telephone the resort tourist office and ask them to send you their information pack. You will find that nearly all the tourist offices have staff that speak English and the brochures will have English translations.

The telephone codes are as follows:

Austria - tel: 010 43
France - tel: 010 33
Swiss - tel: 010 41
Italy - tel: 010 39

Skiing in America

I have not included any American resorts in the report as I don't recommend taking young children to ski in America simply because of the travelling time involved. But if you should decide to go and ski Stateside then you will find the facilities for children quite excellent. The Americans are very geared up for children and you'll find their organisation hard to beat. There'll never be a problem with the language or difficulty finding something the children will like to eat.

The height of the resort and time of year must be taken into consideration because it is not uncommon in Dec/Jan to experience temperatures of -25C. Although the skiing does not generally go much higher than Europe, many resorts in Colorado have a town level of over 8,000ft, which can cause altitude sickness (see chapter on Health).

Here's a brief outline of children's facilities in some American resorts:

Aspen: Snowpuppies - for children from three to six years old.

Breckenridge: Peak 8 and 9 Children's centre - two months to five years. Special ski school for three year olds.

Copper Mountain: The Belly Button Babies/Bakery - three years and over. Infant and Toddler Care - two months and over.

Keystone: Keystone Mountain's Children Centre for children from 2 months to 12 years.

Steamboat Springs: Nursery - six months to six years. Kiddie Corral for toddlers.

Vail: Children's Mountain - 15 acres (just for kids) of teepee villages, gold mines and a fort to ski through. Small World Play School - programmes for babies and toddlers.

■ **It'll all have been worth it when you can ski *en famille***

Picture: Larry Pierce, Steamboat Ski Resort. Courtesy Colorado Tourism Board.

Resort Report

Austria

Alpbach 1000m

GENERAL SKI INFORMATION
Top height: 2025m
Pistes (km): 40
Lifts: 22
Snow-making: Yes
Language: German

LIFT PASSES
Adult 6-day pass: 1210AS
Under 15s 6-day pass: 770AS
Free up to the age of 6 years if skiing with parents.

SKI SCHOOLS
The Schischüle Alpbach Tirol

SCHISCHULE ALPBACH TIROL
Age: 4 years and over
Days: Mon to Sat
Hours: 10am to 12 noon and 1.30pm to 3.30pm
English-speaking ski instructors: 100%
Maximum in ski class: 10
Organised indoor recreation if weather bad: Yes
Supervised lunches: Yes
Prices: 6-days - 1150AS
NB – Reductions available if more than one child of a family in ski school.

SKI KINDERGARTEN
Age: 4 years and over
Days: Mon to Sat
Hours: 9.30am to 4.15pm
English speaking instructors: 100%
Supervised lunch: Yes
Location: Centre of Alpbach
Yes
Prices: 6-days including lunch – 1750AS. Information and registration at the ski school

NURSERY
Age: 3 to 6 years
Days: Mon to Sat
Hours: 9.15am to 4.15pm
Facilities to play outside: No, but weather permitting, the children are taken for walks and tobogganing.
Supervised lunch: Yes
Location: 200m from centre of town. Information and registration at the Tourist Office.
Prices: Per day – 150AS. Half-day – 75AS. Lunch if required 50AS

BABYSITTING
General babysitting: The Tourist Office has a list of girls.
Price: Approx 90AS – 120AS per hour
Hotels with nursery facilities: No

NON-SKIING ACTIVITIES
Sleigh-rides, tobogganing, swimming, skating, and curling (although the last three are a long walk from the village centre).

CLOSEST AIRPORT
Munich – 1½ hours by coach (130km)
Salzburg – (120 km) 1½ hours by coach

TOUR OPERATORS
Neilson

IMPORTANT TELEPHONE NUMBERS
Tourist Office: 53 36 5211
Fax: 53 36 5012
Doctor: Dr Thurner – 53 56 5040

Verdict: Sunny nursery slopes in village, but main skiing is a 5 min bus ride. Not recommended for children under three.

St. Anton 1300m

GENERAL SKI INFORMATION
Top height: 2650m
Pistes (km): 200
Snow-making: Yes
Lifts: 86
Language: German
Ski Club rep

LIFT PASSES
Adult 6-day pass 1840AS
7 to 15 years 6-day pass 1190AS
'Snowman Pass' is available for children of 7 years and under (born after November 15th 1986, proof is required) for 100AS and is valid for the whole season.

SKI SCHOOLS
Arlberg Ski School – 54 46 23 06
Franz Klimmer Ski School – 54 46 35 63

ARLBERG SKI SCHOOL
Age: 5 to 14 years
Days: Sun to Fri
Ski school hours: 9am to 4.30pm
English speaking instructors: 100%
Maximum in ski class: 11
Indoor recreation if weather bad: No
Supervised lunch: Yes
Prices: 6 days with lunch and drink 2030AS

KINDERGARTEN SKI SCHOOL
Age: 2 to 5 years (children must be out of nappies).
Days: Sun to Fri
Hours: 9.30am to 4.30pm
English speaking instructors: 100%
Supervised lunch: Yes
Ratio of children to instructor: 8:1
Location: Arlberg Ski School
Indoor recreation in bad weather: Yes

Price: Approx 2000AS

NURSERY
Age: 2 to 5 years
Days: Sun to Fri
Hours: 9am to 4.30pm
English speaking guardian: Yes
Facilities to play outside: Yes
Supervised lunch: Yes
Location: Town centre
Price: One day 250AS, 6 days with lunch and snacks 980AS.

BABYSITTING
General babysitting: Ask at the Tourist Office
Hotels with nursery facilities:
Hotel Arlberg Hospiz (St Christoph) – 54 46 26 11, free kindergarten to hotel guests only. Hotel Club Aldiana – 54 46 26 21 Hotel Neue Post – 54 46 22 13
Hotel St Christoph – 54 46 36 66

NON-SKIING ACTIVITIES
Indoor swimming pool, squash, tennis, bowling, museum, outdoor skating rink, curling, tobogganing and horse-drawn sleigh rides.

CLOSEST AIRPORT
Munich – 3hrs
Zurich – 3hrs

TOUR OPERATORS
Bladon Lines, Crystal, Enterprise, Inghams, Made to Measure, Mark Warner, Neilson, Ski Club of Great Britain, Supertravel, Thomson.

IMPORTANT TELEPHONE NUMBERS
Tourist Office: 54 46 22 690
Fax: 54 46 25 32 15
Doctor: Dr Knierzinger – 54 46 21 61

Verdict: Although one of the world's great resorts, there's too much walking involved for young children.

BADGASTEIN 1080m

GENERAL SKI INFORMATION
Top height: 2686m
Pistes (km): 250
Lifts: 52
Snow-making: Yes
Language: German

LIFT PASSES
Adult 6-day pass 1680AS
Under 15s 6-day pass 1010AS
Some of the lifts on the nursery
slopes are free for under 6s

SKI SCHOOL
Werner Pflaum – 64 34 22 60
Schischüle Luigi – 64 34 44 40

WERNER PFLAUM SKI SCHOOL
Age: 5 to 14 years
Days: 6 days
Hours: 10am to 12 noon and 1pm to 4pm
English speaking instructors: 100%
Maximum in ski class: 10
Indoor recreation if weather bad: No
Supervised lunch: Yes
Prices: 6 days without lunch 1450AS

KINDERGARTEN SKI SCHOOL
Werner Pflaum
Age: 3 to 5 years
Days: 6 days
Hours: 10am to 4.30pm
English speaking instructors: 100%
Supervised lunch: Yes
Ratio of children to instructor: 6:1
Location: 10 minutes from centre
Indoor recreation if weather bad: Yes
Prices: 6 days with lunch 2000AS

NURSERY – 64 34 25 160
Mini-Club at Grüner Baum Hotel
Age: 3 to 15 years
Days: Daily
Hours: 9.30am to 4.30pm
English speaking guardian: Yes
Facilities to play outside: Yes and ski with instructor
Supervised lunch: Yes
Location: 3kms from town, but children can be collected and delivered by prior arrangement.
Prices: Non-resident at hotel: One day inc skiing and lunch 300AS, 6 days inc skiing and lunch 1500AS.

BABYSITTING
General babysitting: List available at the Tourist Office
Price: Approx 100AS
Hotels with nursery facilities: Grüner Baum

NON-SKIING ACTIVITIES
Indoor swimming, solarium, tennis, squash, cinema, ice-skating, curling, horse drawn sleigh rides, horse back riding, fitness centre, tobogganing.

CLOSEST AIRPORT
Salzburg – 1½ hrs

TOUR OPERATORS
Inghams, Made to Measure, Thomson.

IMPORTANT TELEPHONE NUMBERS
Tourist Office: 64 34 25 31
Fax: 64 34 25 31
Doctor: Dr. Mayerhofer – 64 34 24 93

Verdict: Good resort for experienced skiers with children. Grüner Baum Club is highly recommended.

GENERAL SKI INFORMATION
Top height: 2000m
Pistes (km): 35
Lifts: 40
Snow-making: No
Language: German

LIFT PASSES
Adult 6-day pass 1685AS
Under 15s 6-day pass 1040AS
Free pass up to the age of 5 years

SKI SCHOOL – 55 57 64 01
Age: 6 years and over
Days: Mon to Fri
Hours: 10am to 12 noon and 1pm to 3pm
English speaking instructors: 80%
Maximum in ski class: 12
Indoor recreation if weather bad: No
Supervised lunch: Yes
Prices: 5 days 1050AS
10AS per day for lunch

KINDERGARTEN SKI SCHOOL
Tel: 55 57 64 01
Age: 4 years and over
Days: Mon to Fri
Hours: 9.15am to 3.30pm
English speaking instructors: 100%
Supervised lunch: Yes
Ratio of children to instructor: 8:1
Location: 2 minutes walk from town centre
Indoor recreation if weather bad: Yes
Prices: One day 75AS inc lunch, 20AS for lunchtime supervision.

NURSERY
Tel: 55 57 64 01
Age: From 2 ½ years

Days: Mon to Fri
Hours: 9.15am to 12 noon and 12 noon to 3.30pm
English speaking guardian: Yes
Facilities to play outside: Yes
Supervised lunch: Yes
Location: Town centre next to main chair lift
Prices: One day with lunch 75AS, 12 noon to 3.30pm 20AS

BABYSITTING
There are no babysitting facilities or any hotels with this facility, but ask at your hotel or the Tourist Office who will try to help.

NON-SKIING ACTIVITIES
Tobogganing, paragliding

CLOSEST AIRPORT
Zurich – 2 hrs

TOUR OPERATORS
The Tourist Office were unable to confirm which companies would be operating in Gargellen this winter.

IMPORTANT TELEPHONE NUMBERS
Tourist Office: 55 57 63 03
Fax: 55 57 66 90
Doctor: Dr Tagwercher – 55 56 26 66

Verdict: **Small, friendly resort with gentle runs. Good children's facilities.**

KAPRUN 770 m

GENERAL SKI INFORMATION
Top height: 3029m
Pistes (km): 130 (including Zell am See)
Lifts: 54 (including Zell am See)
Language: German

LIFT PASSES
Adult 6-day pass 1760AS
Under 16s 6-day pass 1090AS
Free pass up to the age of 7 years.

SKI SCHOOL
Kaprun Ski School – 65 47 82 38 0

KAPRUN SKI SCHOOL
Age: 4 years upwards
Days: Sun and Mon to Fri
Hours: 2 hrs am and 2hrs pm
English speaking instructors: 100%
Maximum in ski class: 12
Indoor recreation if weather bad: Yes
Supervised lunch: Yes
Prices: 6-days 1260AS without lunch

KINDERGARTEN SKI SCHOOL
Age: 4 years and over
Days: 6 days a week
Hours: 9am to 5pm
English speaking instructors: 100%
Supervised lunch: Yes
Ratio of children to instructor: 10:1
Location: 50m from town centre
Indoor recreation if weather bad: Yes
Prices: 6 days with lunch 1500AS
NB: The trained children's instructors have a whole ski plus play pro-

gramme for your child. There is also a children's ski lift, play field and fantasy land and every child is filmed on video in the ski school race.

NURSERY
Age: 2 years and over
Days: Sun to Fri
Hours: 9am to 5pm
Facilities to play outside: Yes
English-speaking guardian: Yes
Supervised lunch: Yes
Location: Centre of town
Prices: Approx 1000AS per week

BABYSITTING
General babysitting: List of available babysitters held at Tourist Office.
Prices: 70/80AS per hour
Hotels with nursery facilities: No

NON-SKIING ACTIVITIES
Indoor/outdoor swimming pool, sauna, solarium and steam bath at the Optimum Leisure Centre, squash, tennis, ice-skating, curling, ice-skittles, horse drawn sleigh rides, tobogganing.

CLOSEST AIRPORT
Salzburg – 1 hour

TOUR OPERATORS
Crystal, Enterprise, Made to Measure.

IMPORTANT TELEPHONE NUMBERS
Tourist Office: 65 47 8643
Doctor: Dr Karl Watschinger – 65 478698

Verdict: Good ski kindergarten. Suitable resort for children of all ages except babies.

GENERAL SKI INFORMATION
Top height: 2000m
Pistes (km): 180
Lifts: 63
Snow-making: No
Language: German
Ski Club rep

LIFT PASSES
Adult 6-day pass 1650AS
Under 15s 6-day pass 825AS

SKI SCHOOLS
Ski School Hahnenkamm – 5356 3177
Ski School Kitzbühel Red Devils – 5356 2500
Ski School Total – 5356 72011
Kitzbüheler Horn Ski School – 5356 72591

HAHNENKAMM SKI SCHOOL
Age: 4 to 15 years
Days: Mon to Sat
Hours: Flexible, but generally 9.30am to 12 noon and 1pm to 3pm
English speaking instructors: 100%
Maximum in class: 7, special emphasis is placed on this factor to ensure personal tuition and maximum safety.
Indoor recreation if weather bad: Yes
Supervised lunch: Yes
Location: Office and meeting place behind the Park Hotel, which can be reached through the Hahnenkamm car park. If required children can be collected and returned in the Ski School's own bus.
Prices: 6 days 1800AS plus 80AS for lunch
NB: There are nursery slopes, a chil-

dren's 'fairyland' for all the ski schools and children's races with prizegiving.

KINDERGARTEN SKI SCHOOL
Age: 3 years and over
Days: Daily
Hours: Same as Ski School
English speaking instructors: 100%
Supervised lunch: Yes
Ratio of children to instructor: 15:1
Location: 5 minutes walk from town centre
Indoor recreation if weather bad: Yes
Prices: 6 days 1800AS, 80AS for lunch.

NURSERY – Frau Heckenberger – 5356 3529
Takes babies to 4 years at her own home, Mon to Fri, 8am to 4pm. 400AS per day with lunch. 80AS per hour.
Sometimes available Sat and Sun.
Limited space so book early.

BABYSITTING
General babysitting: List available from Tourist Office
Prices: Approx 100AS per hour
Hotels with nursery facilities:
Four-star Hotel Schlöss Ledenberg – 5456 4301 – Supervised playroom for 3 years and over, 9am to 4pm. Residents only, for which this service is free.

NON-SKIING ACTIVITIES
Two indoor swimming pools, sauna, solarium, mud baths, aerated baths and under-water massage at the Aquarena Centre, indoor tennis, squash, fitness centre, bowling, ice-

skating, curling, hang gliding, horse
riding, horse drawn sleigh rides,
tobogganing, ski-bobs, casino,
wildlife park, ballooning.

CLOSEST AIRPORTS
Salzburg – 1 ½ hrs
Munich – 2 hours

TOUR OPERATORS
Crystal, Enterprise, Inghams, Made
to Measure, Neilson,
Supertravel, Thomson.

IMPORTANT TELEPHONE NUMBERS
Tourist Office: 5356 2155
Fax: 5356 2307
Doctor: Dr Fuchs – 5356 4779
Dr Penz – 5356 5447
(paediatricians)

Verdict: Very popular with the British. Good facilities. Recommended for children.

GENERAL SKI INFORMATION
Top height: 2450m
Lifts: 77 (with Zürs, St Anton)
Snow-making: Yes
Language: German

LIFT PASSES
Adult 6-day pass 1840AS
Under 15s 6-day pass 1100AS
Free pass up to age of 7 years
'Snowman Pass' for children up to 6
years 100AS for whole season.

LECH & OBERLECH SKI SCHOOL
Tel: 55 83 20 07
Age: 6 years and over
Days: Sun to Fri
Hours: 10am to 12 noon and 2pm to 4pm
English speaking instructors: 95%
Maximum in ski class: 10
Indoor recreation if weather bad: No
Supervised lunch: Yes
Prices: 6 days 1290AS

KINDERGARTEN SKI SCHOOL
Tel: 55 83 21 61
Age: From 2½ (provided your child no longer wears nappies)
Days: Sun to Fri
Hours: 9am to 4pm
English speaking instructors: 95%
Ratio of children to instructor: 6:1
Supervised lunch: Yes
Location: Town centre
Organised indoor recreation if weather bad: Yes
Prices: 6 days 1290AS
2 hrs per day 80AS

NURSERY
Info as for kindergarten. Children will be given ski lessons if strong enough, alternatively they will play indoors and go for walks and tobog-ganing. Located 3 minute walk from town centre.

BABYSITTING
General babysitting: A list is available from the Tourist Office
Prices: Approx 100/120AS per hour.
Hotels with supervised nursery facilities: Hotel Goldener Berg (Oberlech) – 55 83 2205/0. Residents only. From 2½ years. 9am to 5pm. Free with lunch extra. Hotel Hinterwies – 55 83 2531. Hotel Rote Wand – 55 83 3435, 9am to 6pm, normally from 2 years, but younger arranged. German nanny. Service free. Hotel Sonnenburg – 55 83 2147. Residents only. From 2 to 10 years. 10am to 12 noon and 2pm to 4pm. No supervised lunch. Babysitters available.

NON-SKIING ACTIVITIES
Indoor tennis, squash, swimming pool and sauna, outdoor natural skating ring, curling, sleigh rides.

CLOSEST AIRPORT
Zurich – 2½ hrs
Munich – 3 hrs

TOUR OPERATORS
Bladon Lines, Inghams

IMPORTANT TELEPHONE NUMBERS
Tourist office: 55 83 21610
Fax: 55 83 3155
Doctor: 55 83 2032

Verdict: Lech is a very *chic* resort but Oberlech is quieter for families.

MAYRHOFEN 1650m

GENERAL SKI INFORMATION
Top height: 2250m
Pistes (km): 90 km
Lifts: 31
Snow-making: Yes
Language: German
Ski Club rep

LIFT PASSES
Adult 6-day pass 1450AS
Under 14s 6-day pass 870AS
Free pass up to the age of 6 years

SKI SCHOOLS
Speiss – 5285 27 95
Garger – 5285 38 00
Rahm – 5285 39 39

SPEISS SKI SCHOOL
Age: 4 to 14 years
Days: Sun and Mon for 6 days
Hours: 10am to 12 noon and 1.30pm
to 3.30pm
English speaking instructors: 100%
Maximum in class: 12
Indoor recreation if weather
bad: Yes
Supervised lunch: Yes (up to the
age of 12).
Location: Office opp. Penken cable
car station.
Prices: 6 days without lunch
1300AS

KINDERGARTEN SKI SCHOOL
Age: 4 to 12 years
Days: Sun to Fri
Hours: 9am to 4pm
English speaking instructors:100%
Supervised lunch: Yes
Ratio of children to instructor:
10:1
Location: Town centre

Indoor recreation if weather
bad: Yes
Prices: 6 days with lunch 1900AS

NURSERY
Wuppys
Age: 3 months to 7 years
Days: Sun to Fri
Hours: 8am to 6pm
English speaking guardian: Yes
Facilities to play outside: Yes
Supervised lunch: Yes
Location: 2 mins from Tourist Office
Prices: 6 days 1500AS, one day
300AS, half-day 150AS, lunch per
day 50AS.

BABYSITTING
General babysitting: List available
at Tourist Office
Prices: 80/100AS per hour
Hotels with nursery facilities: No

NON-SKIING ACTIVITIES
Ice-skating, horse-drawn sleigh
rides, curling, tobogganing, fun-pool
offers fun park with special kid's
area and aquaslide, sauna, massage,
whirlpool and crazy mixer, bowling
and indoor tennis.

CLOSEST AIRPORT
Munich - 2hrs
Innsbruck – 1hr

TOUR OPERATORS
Crystal, Enterprise, Inghams, Made
to Measure, Neilson, Thomson.

IMPORTANT TELEPHONE NUMBERS
Tourist Office: 52 85 23 05
Fax: 52 85 23 05 33
Doctor: Dr Gredler – 52 85 25 50

Verdict: Very popular with the British. Excellent facilities for children.

GENERAL SKI INFORMATION
Top height: 1900m
Pistes (km): 45
Lifts: 33
Snow-making: No
Language: German

LIFT PASSES
Wildschönau pass covers all lifts in Niederau, Oberau and Auffach.
Adult 6-day pass 1280AS
Under 15s 6-day pass 770AS

WILDSCHÖNAU SKI SCHOOL
Tel: 53 39 82 00
Age: 4 to 15 years
Days: Sun to Fri
Hours: 10am to 12 noon and 2pm to 4pm
English speaking instructors: 90%
Maximum in class: 15
Organised indoor recreation if weather bad: Yes
Supervised lunch: Yes
Prices: 6-days 1100AS

KINDERGARTEN SKI SCHOOL
Age: 4 years and over
Days: Sun to Fri
Hours: 10am to 12 noon and 2pm to 4pm
English speaking instructors: 100%
Supervised lunch: Yes
Ratio of children to instructor: 10:1
Location: 500m from town centre
Indoor recreation if weather bad: Yes
Prices: 6 days without lunch 2100AS, lunch110AS per day
15% reduction for children if parent is also taking lessons.
There is a Special Skiing Card, price 250AS for 4 and 5 year olds to try skiing for just one day

NURSERY
Age: 2 to 6 years
Days: Sun to Fri
Hours: 9.30am to 4.30pm
English speaking guardian: Yes
Facilities to play outside: Yes
Supervised lunch: Yes
Location: Town centre
Prices: One day with lunch 280AS. One day without lunch 170AS.

BABYSITTING
General babysitting: No actual list held at the Tourist Office but they will try and help
Prices: Negotiable
Hotels with nursery facilities: None

NON-SKIING ACTIVITIES
Sauna and solarium, bowling, sleigh rides, skating, curling, tobogganing, horse-riding.

CLOSEST AIRPORT
Salzburg – 2 hrs
Munich – 2 hrs

TOUR OPERATORS
Enterprise, Inghams, Neilson, Thomson.

IMPORTANT TELEPHONE NUMBERS
Tourist Office: 53 39 82 55
Fax: 53 39 24 33
Doctor: Dr Lanner – 53 39 83 67

Verdict: Small friendly village. Nursery slopes in town. Recommended.

OBERGURGL 1930m

GENERAL SKI INFORMATION
Top height: 3035m
Pistes (km): 110
Lifts: 23
Snow-making: Yes
Language: German
Ski Club rep

LIFT PASSES
Adult 6-day pass 2030AS
Under 15s 6-day pass 1240AS
Free pass up to age of 6 years

SKI SCHOOL
Obergurgl Ski School – 52 56 305

OBERGURGL SKI SCHOOL
Age: 5 years and over
Days: Sun to Mon for 5 or 6 days
Hours: 10am to 12 noon and 2pm to 4pm
English speaking instructors: 80%
Maximum in class: 13
Indoor recreation if weather bad: No
Supervised lunch: Yes
Prices: 6 days inc lunchtime supervision 1240AS plus 360AS for lunch.

KINDERGARTEN SKI SCHOOL – No

NURSERY
Age: 2 years and over
Days: Daily
Hours: 9.30am to 12.30pm and 1.30pm to 4.30pm
Facilities to play outside: Children are taken for walks
English speaking guardian: Yes
Supervised lunch: Yes, worked in conjunction with Ski School.
Location: Town centre
Prices: Same as ski school

BABYSITTING
General babysitting: No
Hotels with nursery facilities: Hotel Alpina – 52 56 505, Hotel Hochgurgl – 52 56 365, Hotel Austria – 52 56 282, Hotel Bellevue – 52 56 228

NON-SKIING ACTIVITIES
Indoor public and hotel pools, saunas, whirlpools, steam baths, bowling, billiards, squash, table tennis, shooting range, outdoor skating rink, curling, sleigh rides.

CLOSEST AIRPORT
Innsbruck – 2 hrs

TOUR OPERATORS
Bladon Lines, Crystal, Inghams, Made to Measure, Neilson, Supertravel, Thomson.

IMPORTANT TELEPHONE NUMBERS
Tourist Office: 52 56 258/353
Fax: 52 56 333 77
Doctor: Dr Schege – 52 56 229

Verdict: Good resort for late and early holidays, but can be very cold in Dec/Jan.

GENERAL SKI INFORMATION
Top height: 2096m
Pistes (km): 200
Lifts: 60 (Saalbach/Hinterglemm and Leogang)
Snow-making: Yes
Language: German

LIFT PASSES
Covers lifts in Saalbach, Hinterglemm & Leogang and ski bus.
Adult 6-day pass 1700AS
11 to 15 year old 6-day pass 1010AS
6 to 10 year old 6-day pass 750 AS
Free pass up to age of 6 years

SKI SCHOOLS
Saalbach
Willie Fritzenwallner – 65 41 246
Hannes Furstauer – 65 41 84 44
Hans Hinterholzer – 65 41 76 07
Wolfgang Zink – 65 41 84 20
Hinterglemm
Bartl Gensbichler – 65 41 84 44
Lechner – 65 41 73 28
Wolf – 65 41 84 20
Mitterlengau – 64 72 33 33

SKI SCHOOL – Willie Fritzenwallner and Bartl Gensbichler
Age: 4 years and over
Days: Sun to Fri
Hours: 10am to 12 noon and 2pm to 4pm
English speaking instructors: 100%
Maximum in class: 12
Indoor recreation if weather bad: No
Supervised lunch: Yes
Prices: 6 days1350AS

WOLF SKIING AND NON-SKIING KINDERGARTEN HINTERGLEMM ONLY
Age: 2 years and over
Days: Sun to Fri
Hours: 9.30am to 4.30pm
English speaking instructors: Not guaranteed
Supervised lunch: Yes
Facilities to play outside: Yes
Location: Hotel Wolf
Indoor recreation: Yes
Prices: One day 450 AS, 4 to 6 days 1350AS. Lunch per day100AS.

NURSERY – No

BABYSITTING
General babysitting: List available at the Tourist Office
Prices: Approx 100AS per hour
Hotels with nursery facilities:
Hotel Theresia – 7414-0 – Mon to Fri, 9.45am to 4.15am for children over 3 years, hotel residents only.
Aparthotel Adler – 7331-0, from 3 years for 6 days a week.

NON-SKIING ACTIVITIES
Indoor swimming pool, sauna, massage, solarium, bowling, billiards, squash and tennis. Outdoor skating, curling, tobogganing and sleigh rides.

CLOSEST AIRPORT
Saltzburg – 1½ hours

TOUR OPERATORS
Crystal, Enterprise, Ingham, Made to Measure, Neilson, Ski-Tal, Thomson.

IMPORTANT TELEPHONE NUMBERS
Tourist Office: 65 41 72 72
Fax: 65 41 79 00
Doctor: Dr. Ulf Scheuch – 65 41 287 (Saalbach) – Dr. K. Schnell – 65 41 7878 – (Hinterglemm)

Verdict: Hinterglemm has more to offer young children than Saalbach.

SEEFELD 1200m

GENERAL SKI INFORMATION
Top height: 2074m
Pistes (km): 21
Lifts: 20
Snow-making: Yes
Language: German

LIFT PASSES
Adult 6-day pass 1500AS
Under 15s 6-day pass 1140AS
Free pass up to the age of 10 if accompanied by parents.

SKI SCHOOL
Seefeld Ski school – 52 12 24 12

SKI SCHOOL
Age: 4 years and over
Days: Mon to Sat
Hours: 10am to 12 noon and 2pm to 4pm
English speaking instructors: 95%
Maximum in class: 10
Indoor recreation if weather bad: Yes
Supervised lunch: Yes
Prices: 6 days 1190AS plus 100AS per day for lunch.

KINDERGARTEN SKI SCHOOL
Age: 3 ½ years and over
Days: Mon to Sat
Hours: 10am to 4pm
English speaking instructors: 95%
Supervised lunch: Yes
Ratio of children to instructor: 10:1
Location: Town centre
Indoor recreation if weather bad: Yes
Prices: 6 days 1190AS plus 100AS per day for lunch

NURSERY – No

BABYSITTING
General babysitting: A list is available from the Tourist Office
Prices: Approx 70AS to 100AS per hour
Hotels with supervised nursery facilities: (for residents only)
Hotel Waldhotel – 52 12 22 07 – 7 hrs per day. From 3 years.
Hotel Kaltschmid – 52 12 2119 – afternoons only. From 3 years.
Hotel Tummlerhof – 52 12 25 71 – Kinderclub. From 3 years.

NON-SKIING ACTIVITIES
Swimming, saunas, tennis, squash, bowling, tobogganing, skating, curling, horse-riding, sleigh rides, paragliding.

CLOSEST AIRPORT
Innsbruck – 1 hr
Munich – 2 hrs

TOUR OPERATORS
Crystal, Enterprise, Inghams, Thomson.

IMPORTANT TELEPHONE NUMBERS
Tourist Office: 52 12 23 13
Fax: 52 12 33 55
Doctor: Dr Jenelin 52 12 23 88

Verdict: Large Austrian town. Try and stay centrally to avoid walking.

GENERAL SKI INFORMATION
Top height: 3056m
Pistes (km): 100
Lifts: 37
Snow-making: Yes
Language: German

LIFT PASSES
Adult 6-day pass 1850AS
6 to 14 years 6-day pass 1060AS
Free pass up to age of 6 years

SKI SCHOOL
Sölden Ski School – 52 54 23 64

SÖLDEN SKI SCHOOL
Age: 5 years and over
Days: Mon to Sat
Hours: 10am to 12 noon and 1pm to 3pm
English speaking instructors: 90%
Maximum in class: 8 to 10
Indoor recreation if weather bad: Yes
Supervised lunch: No
Prices: 6 days tuition 1290AS

KINDERGARTEN SKI SCHOOL
Age: 3 to 8 years
Days: Mon to Sat
Hours: 9am to 3.30pm
English speaking instructors: 90%
Supervised lunch: Yes
Ratio of children to teacher: 8:1
Location: Town centre
Indoor recreation if weather bad: Yes
Prices: 6 days1590AS (inc lunch)
NB The Kindergarten Ski School may take children under 3 providing they are out of nappies.

NURSERY – No

BABYSITTING
General babysitting: Tourist Office can assist in organising a babysitter, but require plenty of warning.
Prices: Approx 100AS per hour
Hotels with nursery facilities:
Hotel Schöne Aussicht – 54 24 03 – 0-3 years 300AS per day, 3 years and over, free. Normally residents only, but will try to accommodate non-residents if they have space. Hotel Edelweiss – 54 22 98 – 8am to 12 noon Mon to Fri. Free for residents only.

NON-SKIING ACTIVITIES
Indoor swimming pool, sauna, solarium, gym, bowling, tennis, shooting and cinema. Outdoor skating rink, curling, riding and tobogganing.

CLOSEST AIRPORT
Innsbruck – 2 hrs
Munich – 4 hrs

TOUR OPERATORS
Crystal, Inghams, Made to Measure, Neilson, Thomson.

IMPORTANT TELEPHONE NUMBERS
Tourist Office: 52 54 22120
Fax: 52 54 3131
Doctor: Dr. Wutscher – 52 54 22 07

Verdict: Large town with heavy traffic.

WESTENDORF 970m

GENERAL SKI INFORMATION
Top height: 2000m
Pistes (km): 40
Lifts: 14
Snow-making: Yes
Language: German

LIFT PASSES
Children 5 to 14 years 6-day pass 700AS
Free pass up to the age of 5 years.

SKI SCHOOLS
Westendorf - 53 34 61 81
Top Ski school - 53 34 67 37

SKI SCHOOLS – Both
Age: 6 years and over
Days: 6 days
Hours: 10am to 12 noon and 2pm to 4pm
English speaking instructors: 80%
Maximum in class: 12
Indoor recreation if weather bad: No
Supervised lunch: Yes
Prices: 6 days 1150AS, lunch 90AS per day.

KINDERGARTEN SKI SCHOOL
Both ski schools
Age: 4 years and over
Days: 6 days
Hours: 10am to 12 noon and 2pm to 6pm
English speaking instructors: 70%
Supervised lunch: Yes
Ratio of children to instructor: 8:1
Location: Town centre
Indoor recreation if weather bad: Yes
Prices: Same as ski school

NURSERY
Guest Kindergarten Westendorf
Tel: 53 34 61 81
Age: 2 years and over
Days: Sun to Fri
Hours: 9.30am to 12 noon and 1.20pm to 4.30pm
English speaking guardian: Yes
Facilities to play outside: No
Supervised lunch: Yes
Location: Town centre
Prices: One day 250AS, half-day 150AS, lunch 60AS per day.

BABYSITTING
General babysitting: Arrange well in advance with the Tourist Office
Prices: 90/100AS per hour
Hotels with nursery facilities: No

NON-SKIING ACTIVITIES
Ice-skating, bowling, horse-drawn sleighs, walking.

CLOSEST AIRPORT
Innsbruck - 1 ½ hrs
Salzburg - 2 hrs

TOUR OPERATORS
Crystal, Enterprise, Inghams, Neilson, Thomson.

IMPORTANT TELEPHONE NUMBERS
Tourist Office: 53 34 62 30
Fax: 53 34 23 90
Doctor: Dr Graser – 53 34 67 27

Verdict: Recommended for families.

GENERAL SKI INFORMATION
Top height: 1965m
Pistes (km): 130
Lifts: 55
Snow-making: Yes
Language: German

LIFT PASSES
Covers all lifts in Zell and Kaprun and buses between them
Adult 6-day pass 1760AS
Under 15s 6-day pass 1090AS
Free pass up to age of 6 years

SKI SCHOOLS
Schmittenhöhe Ski School – 65 42 3207 or 2715
Wallner-Prenner Ski school – 65 42 2324
Thumersbach Ski school – 65 42 3171 or 3579
Areitbahn Ski school – 65 42 6020

SCHMITTENHÖHE SKI SCHOOL
Age: 4 years and over
Days: Mon to Sun
Hours: 9am to 4.30pm
English speaking instructors: 100%
Maximum in class: 7
Indoor recreation if weather bad: No
Supervised lunch: Yes
Prices: 6 days 1260AS

KINDERGARTEN SKI SCHOOL
Age: 3 years and over
Days: Mon to Sun
Hours: 9am to 4.30pm
English speaking instructors: 100%
Supervised lunch: Yes
Ratio of children to teacher: 10:1

Location: Town centre
Indoor recreation if weather bad: Yes
Prices: 300AS per day

NURSERY – No

BABYSITTING
General babysitting: List available at the Tourist Office
Price: Approx 80AS
Hotels with nursery facilities:
Hotel Movenpick – 65 42 23 88. Children's room which can be supervised for three year olds and over. Free. Strictly for residents only. Hotel can arrange babysitters.

NON-SKIING ACTIVITIES
Indoor swimming pool, sauna, solarium, fitness centre, tennis, squash, bowling, shooting range, museum. Outdoor skating rink, curling, riding, tobogganing, sleigh rides.

CLOSEST AIRPORT
Salzburg – 1 ½ hrs
Munich – 2 hrs

TOUR OPERATORS
Crystal, Enterprise, Inghams, Neilson, Thomson.

IMPORTANT TELEPHONE NUMBERS
Tourist Office: 65 42 2600
Fax: 65 42 2032
Doctor: Medical Centre – 65 42 33 43

Verdict: Attractive, car free centre. Good nursery slopes.

France

GENERAL SKI INFORMATION
Top height: 3330m
Pistes (km): 220
Lifts: 86
Snow-making: Yes
Language: French
Ski Club rep

LIFT PASSES
Adult 6-day pass 870FF
Under 13s 6-day pass 696FF
Free pass up to age of 5 years (proof of age required).
Reductions for families of 4 or more.

SKI SCHOOLS
E.S.F. Ski School – 76 80 31 69
Ski Ecole International – 76 80 42 77

E.S.F. SKI SCHOOL
Age: 3 years and over
Days: Daily
Hours: 9.45am to 12.45pm and 2.30pm to 5pm up until 13.2.93 and then 3pm to 5.30pm
English speaking instructors: 50%
Maximum in class: 7 (13 in French school holidays).
Indoor recreation if weather bad: Yes
Supervised lunch: No
Prices: 6 days 650FF

KINDERGARTEN SKI SCHOOL
Jardin de Neige
Age: 3 years and over
Days: Daily
Hours: 9.45am to 12.45pm and 2.30pm to 5pm
English speaking instructors: 100%
Supervised lunch: No
Ratio of children to instructor: 7:1
Location: 500m from town centre
Indoor recreation if weather bad: Yes
Prices: 6-days 650FF

SKI ÉCOLE INTERNATIONAL
Age: From 3$\frac{1}{2}$ and over
Days: Daily
Hours: 9.30am to 12 noon and 3pm to 5pm
English speaking instructors: 100%
Maximum in class: 8
Indoor recreation if weather bad: Yes
Supervised lunch: No
Prices: 6 days 845 FF

KINDERGARTEN SKI SCHOOL
Tel: 76 80 42 77
Club des Mickeys et Des Papotines
Age: 3 1/2 to 4 years
Club des Marmottes
Age: 5 to 12 years
Days: Daily
Hours: 9.30am to 12 noon and 3pm to 5pm
English speaking instructors: 100%
Supervised lunch: No
Ratio of children to instructor: 8:1
Location: 500m from town centre
Indoor recreation if weather bad: Yes
Prices: Not known at time of going to print but the school estimates approx 845FF for 6 days.

NURSERY

Les Eterlous – 76 80 43 27
Age: 6 months to 14 years
Days: Daily
Hours: 8.30am to 6pm
English speaking guardian: Yes
Facilities to play outside: Yes

Supervised lunch: Yes, but they must take their own.
Location: 10 mins from town centre. Crèche bus will collect and deliver children.
Prices: 205FF per day
NB Children from 2 years can be given ski tuition in the private Les Eterlous area.

BABYSITTING

General babysitting: A list is available from the Tourist Office
Prices: Approx 40FF per hour
Hotels with nursery facilities: Club Med, Club Aquarius.

NON-SKIING ACTIVITIES

Indoor ice skating, curling, sports centre with tennis, gym, squash, aerobics, weight training, climbing wall, sauna, jacuzzi, billiards, outdoor heated swimming pool, shooting range, hang-gliding, paragliding, ice-driving, snow scooters.

CLOSEST AIRPORT

Lyon –3 hrs
Geneva – 3 hrs
Grenoble – 2 hrs

TOUR OPERATORS

Club Med, Crystal, Enterprise, Inghams, Made to Measure, Neilson, Ski Peak, Thomson.

IMPORTANT TELEPHONE NUMBERS

Tourist Office: 76 80 35 41
Fax: 76 80 69 54
Doctor: Group Medical (Dr. Tkatchouk & Dr. Roux) – 76 80 35 84

Verdict: Popular with the British. Open sunny nursery slopes. Can be a lot of walking in resort.

GENERAL SKI INFORMATION
Top height: 3226m
Pistes (km): 150
Lifts: 72
Snow-making: Yes
Language: French
Ski Club rep

LIFT PASSES
Adult 6-day pass 875FF
7 to 12 years 6-day pass 745FF
Free pass up to age of 7 years
10% reduction when buying 3 full-paying passes.

SKI SCHOOLS
E.S.F. French Ski School – Arc 1600
79 07 43 09
Arc 1800 – 79 07 40 31
Arc 2000 – 79 07 47 52
E.S.I. Ski School – 79 41 55 42
Virages Ski School – 79 07 78 82

E.S.F. SKI SCHOOL
Age: 4 years and over
Days: Sun to Fri
Hours: 9.30am to 12 noon and 2pm to 4.30pm
English speaking instructors: 90%
Maximum in ski class: 8
Organised indoor recreation if weather bad: Yes
Supervised lunch: Yes
Prices: 6 days 680FF

KINDERGARTEN SKI SCHOOL
E.S.F. Ski School
Age: 3 years and over
Hours: 8.30am to 6pm (inc. lunch)
Days: Daily
English speaking instructors: 100%

Supervised lunch: Yes
Ratio of children to instructor: Max 15:1
Location: Arc 1800 La Nova Centre
Indoor recreation if weather bad: Yes
Prices: 6 days ski package which includes 4 hours instruction per day, ski equipment, test at end of week and medal 1385FF plus 360FF lunch per week.

E.S.I. SKI SCHOOL
Age: 4 years and over
Hours: 8.30am to 4.30pm
Days: Daily
English speaking instructors: 100%
Supervised lunch: Yes
Ratio of children to instructor: 15:1
Location: 3 minutes from town centre at Residence les Tournevelles
Indoor recreation if weather bad: Yes
Prices: Approx 680FF per week

NB Some of the courses specially run for children by the various ski schools are only available during the French school holidays.

NURSERY
Arc 1600 – Hotel La Cachette – 79 07 70 50
Age: Baby Club – 4 months to 1 year/Grand Baby Club – 1 to 3 years and Mini Club 3 to 7 years
Hours: 8.30am to 6pm
Days: Daily
English speaking guardian: Yes
Facilities to play outside: Yes
Supervised lunch: Yes

Location: Town centre
Prices: Approx 290FF per day with lunch.

Arc 1800 – Nurserie Residence Les Lauzieres
Age: 1 to 3 years
Hours: 8.30am to 6pm
Days: Daily
English speaking guardian: Yes
Facilities to play outside: Yes
Supervised lunch: Yes
Location: Charvet Village
Prices: Mornings or afternoons per week 510FF, full day per week 835FF and 360FF extra per week for lunch.

ARC 1800 – Garderie Residence la Nova
Age: 3 to 8 years
Hours: 8.30am to 6pm
Days: Daily
English speaking guardian: Yes
Facilities to play outside: Yes
Supervised lunch: Yes
Location: Town centre
Prices: 'Ski package' 1385FF per week. 6-full days 810FF. 6-half days 430FF and 360FF for lunch per week.
NB The Residence la Nova runs various 'Clubs', featuring ski instruction, walks and games.
BABYSITTING
General babysitting: List available from Tourist Office
Prices: Approx 50FF per hour
Hotels with nursery facilities:
Hotel Cachette – 79 07 70 50 (see Nursery. Free to hotel guests).

NON-SKIING ACTIVITIES
Squash, sauna, gym, cinema, outdoor skating rink, floodlit skiing, hang-gliding, horse riding, sleigh rides.

CLOSEST AIRPORT
Chambery – 2 ½ hrs
Geneva- 4 ½ hrs

TOUR OPERATORS
Chalets and Hotels "Unlimited", Club Med, Crystal, Enterprise, Made to Measure, Neilson, Thomson.

IMPORTANT TELEPHONE NUMBERS
Tourist Office: 79 41 55 45
Fax: 79 07 45 96
Doctor: Arc 1600 – Dr. Petitot & Dr. Carrere 79 07 78 57
Arc 1800 – Dr. Galeron & Dr. Hoa – 79 07 40 60

Verdict: Mainly self-catering. Children's facilities are conveniently located.

GENERAL SKI INFORMATION
Top height: 2275m
Pistes (km): 650
Lifts: 260
Snow-making: Yes
Language: French
Ski Club rep

LIFT PASSES
Adults 6-day pass 805FF
Under 12s 6-day pass 531FF

SKI SCHOOL
E.S.F. Ski School – 50 74 05 65

SKI SCHOOL
Age: 4 to 12 years
Days: 6 days
Hours: 9.30am to 12 noon and
2.30pm to 5pm
English speaking instructors:
90%
Maximum in class: 10
**Indoor recreation if weather
bad:** No
Supervised lunch: Yes
Prices: Approx 950FF. Lunch extra.

KINDERGARTEN SKI SCHOOL
Children's Village – 50 74 04 46
Age: 3 to 16 years
Days: Daily
Hours: 9am to 5.30pm
English speaking instructors: 80%
Supervised lunch: Yes
Ratio of children to instructor:
10:1
Location: Town centre
**Indoor recreation if weather
bad:** Yes
Prices: 6-days 875FF, lunch 42FF
per day

NURSERY
"Les P'tits Loups" – 50 74 02 11
Age: 3 months to 3 years
Days: Daily
Hours: 9am to 5.30pm
English speaking guardian: Yes
Supervised lunch: Yes
Location: Centre
Prices: 6 days 975FF/6 half-days
550FF, lunch 27FF per day.

BABYSITTING
General babysitting: Ask at
Tourist Office.
Prices: Approx 50FF per hour

NON-SKIING ACTIVITIES
Sauna, jacuzzi, sunbeds, squash,
turkish bath, bowling, outdoor ice-
rink, husky drawn sleigh rides, snow
scooters, hang-gliding, cinema,
tobogganing.

CLOSEST AIRPORT
Geneva – 2 hrs

TOUR OPERATORS
Bladon Lines, Chalets and Hotels
"Unlimited", Club Med, Crystal
Enterprise, Inghams, Made to
Measure, Neilson, Supertravel,
Thomson.

IMPORTANT TELEPHONE NUMBERS
Tourist Office: 50 74 02 11
Fax: 50 74 18 25
Doctor: Medical Centre – 50 74 05 42

Verdict: Purpose built resort. Good for families.

LES CARROZ 1500m

GENERAL SKI INFORMATION
Top height: 2500m
Pistes (km): 260 (with Flaine, Samoens).
Lifts: 30
Snow-making: Yes
Language: French

LIFT PASSES
Adult 6-day pass 605FF, 720FF (with Flaine)
Under 12s 6-day pass 520FF
Free up to the age of 4 years

SKI SCHOOLS
Skinori – 50 90 30 63
E.S.F. – 50 90 02 38
Nouvelle Dimension – 50 90 36 03

SKINORI SKI SCHOOL
Candy Ski Programme
Age: 6 to 12 years
Days: Mon to Sat or Sun to Fri
Hours: 8.45am to 4.30pm
English speaking instructors: 80%
Maximum in class: 12
Indoor recreation if weather bad: Yes
Supervised lunch: No
Prices: 6 half-days 550FF

SKINORI KINDERGARTEN
Age: 3 years to 5 years
Days: Mon to Sat or Sun to Fri
Hours: Mornings or afternoons
English speaking instructors: 80%
Supervised lunch: Yes
Ratio of children to instructor: 12:1
Location: Centre
Indoor recreation if weather bad: Yes
Prices: Half-day 160FF, 6 half-days 680FF

NURSERY
La Souris Verte
Age: 3 months to 5 years
Days: Daily
Hours: 8.45am to 5.30pm
English speaking guardian: Yes
Facilities to play outside: Yes
Supervised lunch: Yes, but children must bring their own.
Location: Town centre
Prices: One hour 34FF, half-day 67FF, one day 135FF, 6 1/2 days 350FF, 6 days 660FF.

BABYSITTING
General babysitting: List available at Tourist Office and nursery.
Prices: Approx 40FF per hour
Hotels with nursery facilities: No

NON-SKIING ACTIVITIES
Paragliding, hang-gliding.

CLOSEST AIRPORT
Geneva – 1½ hrs

TOUR OPERATORS
Enterprise, Total Ski, Ski-Tal.

IMPORTANT TELEPHONE NUMBERS
Tourist Office: 50 90 00 04
Fax: 50 90 07 00
Doctor: Medical Centre – 50 90 07 00

Verdict: Good for families.

GENERAL SKI INFORMATION
Top height: 3790m
Pistes (km): 160
Lifts: 45 (203 Mont Blanc)
Snow-making: Yes
Language: French
Ski Club rep

LIFT PASSES
Adults 6-day pass 860FF
Under 11s 6-day pass 645FF
"Ski Liberty" – Book of 60 coupons at special price of 1350FF allows your entire family to discover the Chamonix Valley.

SKI SCHOOL
E.S.F. Ski School – 50 53 22 57

E.S.F. SKI SCHOOL
Age: 4 to 12 years
Days: Mon to Sat
Hours: 10am to 12 noon and 2pm to 4pm
English speaking instructors: 30%
Maximum in class: 12
Indoor recreation if weather bad: No
Supervised lunch: Yes
Prices: Package One inc lessons (24hr) plus ski rental 820FF

E.S.F. at Argentière – 50 54 00 12
Age: 3 to 12 years
Days: Daily (except Sat in non-hol periods)
Hours: 9am to 5.30pm
English speaking instructors: 50%
Maximum in ski class: 10
Indoor recreation if weather bad: Yes
Supervised lunch: Yes

Prices: Approx 650FF

E.S.F. KINDERGARTEN SKI SCHOOL
Tel: 50 53 22 77
Age: 4 to 12 years
Days: Daily (except Sats in non-hol periods).
Hours: 9am to 5pm
English speaking instructors: Probably
Supervised lunch: Yes
Ratio of children to instructor: 12:1
Location: 200m from centre of town
Indoor recreation if weather bad: No
Prices: Approx 700FF

NURSERY
Day Care Centre – 50 53 12 24
Age: 18 months to 6 years
Days: Daily
Hours: 9am to 6pm
English speaking guardian: Hopefully
Facilities to play outside: No
Supervised lunch: Yes
Location: Centre
Prices: Approx 1200FF

Panda Club
Clos de Savoy – 50 55 86 12
Age: 3 months to three years
Days: Daily
Hours: 8.30am to 5.30pm
English speaking guardian: Yes
Facilities to play outside: Yes
Supervised lunch: Yes
Ratio of children to instructor: 7:1
Prices: Approx 1400FF for 6 days inc lunch.

Panda Club/Panda Ski
Nr Lognan cable car – 50 54 04 76
Age: 3 to 12 years
Days: Daily
Hours: 8.30am to 5.30pm
English speaking instructors: Yes
Facilities to play outside: Yes
Supervised lunch: Yes
Ratio of children to instructor:
10:1
Indoor recreation if weather bad: Yes
Price: Approx 1400FF for 6 days inc lunch

"Vacations without Parents", for 4 to 12 year olds during the school hols only – 50 54 04 76

BABYSITTERS
General babysitting: A list is available from the Tourist Office
Prices: 30/40FF per hour

NON-SKIING ACTIVITIES
Sports Centre (table tennis, fitness, saunas, sunbeds), ice-skating, curling, swimming pool with slide, indoor practice golf, saunas, tennis, squash, fitness centre, Alpine museum, casino, cinemas, tobogganing, snow-shoe walks, ice-driving circuit, horse-riding, hang-gliding, paragliding.

CLOSEST AIRPORT
Geneva – 1 ½ hr

TOUR OPERATORS
Chalets and Hotels "Unlimited", Club Med, Crystal, Enterprise, Inghams, Made to Measure, Neilson, Ski Esprit, Ski-Tal, Thomson,

Ultimate Holidays.

IMPORTANT TELEPHONE NUMBERS
Tourist Office: 50 53 00 24
Fax: 50 53 58 90
Doctor: Dr Destré – 50 53 48 40

Verdict: Good children's facilities but the town is very large andnot ideal for young children.

GENERAL SKI INFORMATION
Top height: 2490m
Pistes (km): 130
Lifts: 56
Snow-making: No
Language: French

LIFT PASSES
Adults 6-day pass 650FF
Under 13s 6-day pass 520FF

E.S.F. SKI SCHOOL
Tel: 50 02 40 83
Age: 5 to 12 years
Days: Mon to Sat
Hours: 9.30am to 11.30am and
2.30pm to 4.30pm
English speaking instructors: 30%
Maximum in class: 12
Indoor recreation if weather bad: No
Supervised lunch: No
Prices: 310FF for 6-half days,
550FF for 5 full-days.

KINDERGARTEN SKI SCHOOL
Club des Champions
Age: 3 ½ to 6 years. From 3 ½
they can learn to ski in the snowgarden and from 5 years old they have
ski lessons on the pistes.
Days: Mon to Sat
Hours: 8.30am to 6pm
English speaking instructors: 70%
Supervised lunch: Yes
Ratio of children to instructor: 10:1
Location: Centre of town
Indoor recreation if weather bad: Yes
Prices: 6 days 587FF, ski tuition is
extra at 40FF per hour, special
weekly rates. During the French
holidays a Ski Plus package is run

for children who hold the 3 star, Mon
to Fri at 1600FF which includes
lunch and care if the weather is bad.

NURSERY
Le Club des Mouflets – 50 02 50 60
Age: 8 months to 4 ½ years
Days: Daily
Hours: 8.30am to 6pm
English speaking guardian:
Hopefully
Facilities to play outside: No
Supervised lunch: Yes, but lunch
must be booked before 10am if
required.
Location: Above Tourist Office
Prices: Same as Club des Champions

BABYSITTERS
General babysitting: A list is
available from the Tourist Office
Prices: Approx 35/40FF per hour
Hotels with nursery facilities: No

NON-SKIING ACTIVITIES
Vitahotel Fitness Centre (swimming
pool), sauna and massage, ice-skating, curling, hang-gliding, paragliding, motor bike circuit, sleigh rides.

CLOSEST AIRPORT
Geneva – 2 hrs

TOUR OPERATORS
Chalets and Hotels "Unlimited",
Crystal, Enterprise, Made to
Measure, Neilson, Ski Esprit, Ski
Total, The Ski Company, Thomson.

IMPORTANT TELEPHONE NUMBERS
Tourist Office: 50 02 60 92
Fax: 50 02 60 92
Doctor: Dr. Pecheur – 50 02 42 63

Verdict: Good all round resort for families. Some walking
involved if not staying in centre, so use bus.

LES COCHES 1450m

GENERAL SKI INFORMATION
Top height: 3250m
Pistes (km): 208 (inc La Plagne)
Lifts: 106 (inc La Plagne)
Snow-making: Yes
Language: French

LIFT PASSES
Adult 6-day pass 875FF
Under 14s 6-day pass 660FF
Free for under 8s from 4.1.93 to 1.2.93
Free pass up to the age of 6 years

SKI SCHOOL
E. S. F. aux Coches – 79 07 80 33

SKI SCHOOL
Age: 4 to 14 years
Days: Sun to Fri
Hours: 10am to 12.30pm and 2pm to 4.30pm
English speaking instructors: 60%
Maximum in class: 8/10
Indoor recreation if weather bad: No
Supervised lunch: No
Prices: 6 days 325FF

KINDERGARTEN SKI SCHOOL
Club Pirouette
Age: 4 to 14 years
Days: Sun to Fri
Hours: 10am to 12.30pm and 2pm to 4.30pm
English speaking instructors: 50%
Supervised lunch: Yes
Ratio of children to instructor: 8:1
Location: Town centre
Indoor recreation if weather bad: Yes
Prices: 6 days inc lunch 850FF, 6 half-days 320FF.

NURSERY
Club Piroutte
Age: 18 months to 8 years
Days: Daily
Hours: 9am to 5.30pm
English speaking guardian: 50%
Facilities to play outside: Yes
Supervised lunch: Yes
Location: Town centre
Prices: 6 days inc lunch 850FF, 6 half-days pm or am 320FF.
This club also offers two evening services "Le Club Fete" on Fridays from 5.30pm to 7pm for 45FF. "Le Club Nuit" on Tuesdays from 7.30pm to 11pm for 90FF (no meals included). NB The Club Pirouette has its own minibus for collecting the children.

BABYSITTING
General babysitting: A list is available from the Tourist Office
Prices: Negotiable
Hotels with nursery facilities: None

NON-SKIING ACTIVITIES
Snow-walking, hang-gliding, floodlit tobogganing, sauna, sunbeds.

Closest airport
Geneva – 4 hrs
Lyon – 4 hrs

TOUR OPERATORS
Ski Esprit, Simply Ski, Crystal.

IMPORTANT TELEPHONE NUMBERS
Tourist Office: 79 07 82 82
Fax: 79 07 80 18
Doctor: Dr. Whitechurch – 79 07 83 59

Verdict: Small hamlet linked to La Plagne with very good children's facilities. Nursery slopes in village.

GENERAL SKI INFORMATION
Top height: 3200m
Pistes (km): 600
Lifts: 190
Snow-making: Yes
Language: French

LIFT PASSES
Adults 6-day pass 960FF (Trois
Vallées).
Under 16s 6-day pass 720FF
Free pass up to 5 years

SKI SCHOOL
E.S.F. Ski School – 79 08 07 72

SKI SCHOOL
Age: 3 years and over
Days: Mon to Sat
Hours: 9am to 12.30pm and 1.30pm
to 4.30pm
English speaking instructors:
English group classes
Maximum in class: 12
**Organised indoor recreation if
weather bad:** Yes
Supervised lunch: Yes
Prices: 6-day class 890FF with
lunch 1125FF

SKIING AND NON-SKIING KINDER-
GARTEN – 79 08 08 47
at 1850m and 1650m
Age: 2 to 13 years
Days: Daily
Hours: 9am to 5pm
English speaking instructors: 80%
Supervised lunch: Yes
Ratio of children to instructor:
8:1 (more in French hols)
Location: Town centre (both)
**Organised indoor recreation if
weather bad:** Yes

Prices: 6 days 890FF, with lunch
1125FF.

BABYSITTING
General babysitting: List available
at Tourist Office
Prices: Approx 50FF per hour
Hotels with nursery facilities:
None

NON-SKIING ACTIVITIES
Indoor ice-rink, squash, swimming
and saunas in hotels, gym, cinema,
games rooms, billiards, hang-gliding,
ski-jumping, paragliding, snow
bikes, floodlit skiing, tobogganing,
snow-shoe walks.

CLOSEST AIRPORT
Chambery – 1 1/2 hrs
Geneva – 3 hrs

TOUR OPERATORS
Bladon Lines, Chalets and Hotels
"Unlimited", Crystal, Enterprise,
Inghams, Le Ski, Made to Measure,
Ski Esprit, Supertravel.

IMPORTANT TELEPHONE NUMBERS
Tourist Office: 79 08 00 29
Fax: 79 08 33 54
Doctor: Medical Centre – 79 08 32 13

Verdict: Highly recommended for family holidays.

LES DEUX ALPES 1650m

GENERAL SKI INFORMATION
Top height: 3600m
Pistes (km): 196
Lifts: 64
Snow-making: Yes
Language: French

LIFT PASSES
Adult 6-day pass 825FF
Under 13s 6-day pass 610FF
4 to 6 years 6-day pass 71FF
Free up to the age of 4 years

SKI SCHOOL
E.S. F. Ski School – 76 79 21 21
École Internationale de Ski de St
Christoph – 76 75 04 21

SKI SCHOOL
**École Internationale de Ski de St
Christoph**
Age: 4 years and over
Days: Sun to Fri or Mon to Sat
Hours: 9.30am to 12 noon and
2.30pm to 5pm
English speaking instructors: 80%
Maximum in class: 10
**Indoor recreation if weather
bad:** No
Supervised lunch: Yes
Prices: 6 mornings 440FF. Lunch
68FF per day.
A free bus is available for children 4
to 6 years.

KINDERGARTEN SKI SCHOOL – both
Jardins des Neiges
Age: 4 to 6 years
Days: Daily
Hours: 9.30am to 12 noon and
2.30pm to 5pm
English speaking instructors: Yes
Supervised lunch: Yes
Ratio of children to instructor: 7:1

Location: 2 in the centre and one at
the entrance of the resort
**Organised indoor recreation if
weather bad:** Yes
Prices: Weekly card, am 500FF,
pm 430FF (from Sun to Fri).

NURSERY
Crèche du Clos des Fonds – 76 79
02 62
Age: 6 months to 2 years
Days: Daily
Hours: 8.30am to 5.30pm
English speaking guardian: Yes
Facilities to play outside: No
Supervised lunch: Yes
Location: "Le Village"
Prices: Approx one day with lunch
170FF, half-day without lunch 90FF.

BABYSITTING
General babysitting: A list is
available from the Tourist Office.
Prices: Approx 40FF per hour
Hotels with nursery facilities: No

NON-SKIING ACTIVITIES
2 swimming pools, 3 fitness centres,
2 bowling alleys.

CLOSEST AIRPORT
Grenoble – 1 ½ hr

TOUR OPERATORS
Bladon Lines, Chalets and Hotels
"Unlimited", Crystal, Enterprise,
Inghams, Made to Measure Neilson,
Ski Club of Great Britain, Thomson

IMPORTANT TELEPHONE NUMBERS
Tourist Office: 76 79 22 00
Fax: 76 79 01 38
Doctor: Dr Bernard – 76 79 20 03

Verdict: Popular with the British. Some good easy skiing
on the glacier. Facilities for babies.

FLAINE 1600m

GENERAL SKI INFORMATION
Top height: 2480m
Pistes (km): 269
Lifts: 80
Snow-making: Yes
Language: French
Ski Club rep

LIFT PASSES
Covers all linked resorts
Free pass up to age of 4 years
Adults 6-day pass 720FF
Under 12s 6-day pass 520FF

SKI SCHOOLS
E.S.F.– 50 90 81 00
Ski École International – 50 90 84 41
Flaine Super Ski – 50 90 82 88 –
8 to 15 year olds

E.S.F. SKI SCHOOL
Age: 4 to 12 years
Days: Sun to Fri
Hours: 2 hours per day, am or pm
English speaking instructors: 100%
Maximum in class: 15
Indoor recreation if weather bad: Yes
Supervised lunch: Yes
Prices: 6 days 350FF, one day 84FF

KINDERGARTEN SKI SCHOOL
RABBIT CLUB AND SKI JUNIOR
Age: 4 to 12 years
Days: Sat to Fri
Hours: 9am to 6pm
English speaking instructors: 100%
Supervised lunch: Yes
Ratio of children to instructor: 10:1
Location: 200m from town centre
Indoor recreation : Yes
Prices: 6 days with lunch 990FF, without lunch 785FF.

NURSERY AND FLAINE JUNIOR
Age: 3 months to 2 years/7 years

Days: Sun to Fri
Hours: 9am to 5pm
English speaking guardian: Yes
Facilities to play outside: Yes
Supervised lunch: Yes
Location: Hotel les Lindars
Prices: A' baby' package is offered for residents which includes cot, nursery supervision and electronic listening device in hotel bedroom at 1900FF per week full board. For non-residents, full day 230FF, lunch 40FF and half day 120FF
NB The nursery is limited to 25 children, priority is given to guests staying at the Hotel les Lindars and advance booking is recommended.
2 to 7 years ski with schools and play.

BABYSITTING
General babysitting: List available from the Tourist Office
Prices: Approx 35FF per hour
Hotels with nursery facilities:
Hotel les Lindars – 50 90 81 66

NON-SKIING ACTIVITIES
Indoor swimming pool, sauna, solarium, gym, cinema, art gallery, ice-rink, hang-gliding, paraskiing, snow-mobiles, snow scooters, ice-driving car-circuit, snow-shoe walking and helicopter rides.

CLOSEST AIRPORT
Geneva – 2 hrs
TOUR OPERATORS
Bladon Lines, Chalets and Hotels "Unlimited", Enterprise, Inghams, Made to Measure, Neilson, Ski Club of Great Britain, Thomson.

IMPORTANT TELEPHONE NUMBERS
Tourist Office: 50 90 80 01
Fax: 50 90 86 26
Doctor: Dr. Joubart – 50 90 81 42

Verdict: What it lacks in alpine charm it certainly makes up for in children's facilities. Recommended.

MEGÈVE 1100m

GENERAL SKI INFORMATION
Top height: 2350m
Pistes (km): 300
Lifts: 82
Snow-making: Yes
Language: French
Ski Club rep

LIFT PASSES
Mont-Blanc pass covers 13 ski
resorts.
Adult 6-day pass 860FF.
Under 12s 6-day pass 645FF.
Mont-Blanc Evasion pass 6-day.
Free pass up to age of 3 years.
Adult 764FF
Under 12s 649FF

SKI SCHOOL
E.S.F. – 50 21 00 97
Age: 5 to 12 years
Days: Sun pm to Sat am
Hours: 9.30am to 11.30am and 3pm
to 5pm
English speaking instructors: 45%
Maximum in class: 12
**Indoor recreation if weather
bad:** No
Supervised lunch: Yes
Prices: Per week 24 hours instruc-
tion 650FF

SKI KINDERGARTEN/NURSERY
Baby Club – Tel 50 58 77 84
Age: 1 to 6 years
Days: Daily
Hours: 8am to 6pm
English speaking guardian: Yes
Facilities to play outside: Yes
Supervised lunch: Yes
Location: Route du Palais des
Sports
Prices: 5 days with lunch 800FF.
190FF per day with lunch. 140FF per
day without lunch.

NB Ski instruction is available if
required at an additional cost

There are several other Kindergartens
offering ski instruction if required in
addition to daily supervision and meals:-
Alpage: 50 21 10 97 – 3 to 6 years ,
9.15am to 5.30pm.
Caboche: 50 58 97 65 – 3 to 10 years ,
9am to 5.30 pm.
Montjoie: 50 21 01 56 – 3 to 13 years,
8.45am to 6pm.
Princesse: 50 93 00 86 – 3 to 6 years,
9am to 5pm.

BABYSITTING
General babysitting: A list of babysit-
ters is available from the Tourist Office
Prices: Approx 35/50FF per hour
Hotels with nursery facilities: No

NON-SKIING ACTIVITIES
Indoor swimming pool, sauna, solarium,
skating, gym, golf driving, judo, dance
classes, bridge, tennis, yoga, archery,
museum, library, cinema, casino, con-
cert hall, outdoor skating rink, horse
riding, sleigh rides, plane and helicopter
trips, paragliding.

CLOSEST AIRPORT
Geneva – 1½ hours

TOUR OPERATORS
Chalets and Hotels "Unlimited",
Crystal, Made to Measure, Ski Esprit,
Supertravel.

IMPORTANT TELEPHONE NUMBERS
Tourist Office: 50 21 27 28
Fax: 50 93 03 09
Doctor: Dr. Lami – 50 58 74 7

Verdict: Attractive car free centre. Wide sunny open
slopes. Good choice of kindergartens.

GENERAL SKI INFORMATION
Top height: 3400m
Pistes (km): 600km (Trois Vallees)
Lifts: 190
Snow-making: Yes
Language: French

LIFT PASSES
Adult 6-day pass 960FF (Trois Vallées).
Under 16s 6-day pass 720FF.
Free pass up to the age of 5 years.

SKI SCHOOL
E.S.F. – 79 08 60 31
Age: 4 years and over
Days: Mon for 5 days or Sun for 6 days
Hours: 9.45am to 12.15pm and 3pm to 5pm (differs during season).
English speaking instructors: 80%
Maximum in class: 15
Indoor recreation if weather bad: No
Supervised lunch: Yes
Prices: 5 days 890FF, supervised lunch 5 days 550F, 6 days 940FF, supervised lunch 660FF.

KINDERGARTEN SKI SCHOOL
Jardin de Ski
Age: 3 to 12 year olds
Days: Daily (Closed Sat and Sun in low season)
Hours: 9.30am to 11.45am and 2.45pm to 5pm
English speaking instructors: Yes
Supervised lunch: Yes
Ratio of children to instructor: 10:1
Location: Rond Point reached by bus or the Rhodos bubble
Indoor recreation if weather bad: Yes
Prices: One day 150FF, 6 days 630FF, supervised lunch per day 120FF.

NURSERY
Club Saturnin 79 08 66 90
Age: 2 to 8 years (Health cert needed for 2 year olds)
Days: Daily
Hours: 9am to 5pm
English speaking guardian: Yes
Facilities to play outside: Yes
Supervised lunch: Yes
Location: Tourist Office, Meribel les Allues.
Prices: 6 days with lunch 1040FF, half-day 77FF.
Children aged three can play on their skis with an instructress in the morning. Must have own skis and boots. At the time of going to print the E.S.F. were unsure if there would be a nursery in Mottaret. The nursery Les Pengouins has closed.

BABYSITTING
General babysitting: List of girls available from the Tourist Office
Prices: Negotiable
Hotels with nursery facilities: No

NON-SKIING ACTIVITIES
Ice-skating, swimming, fitness centre, snowbiking, snow shoe walks, sauna, solarium, jacuzzi, hang-gliding, paragliding, library, astronomy centre, cinema, video club.

CLOSEST AIRPORT
Chambery – 1hr/ Geneva –2 ½ hrs

TOUR OPERATORS
Bladon Lines, Chalets and Hotels "Unlimited", Crystal, Enterprise, Inghams, Made to Measure, Mark Warner, Meriski, Neilson, Ski Peak, Snowtime, Supertravel, Thomson.

IMPORTANT TELEPHONE NUMBERS
Tourist Office: 79 08 60 01
Fax: 79 00 59 61
Doctor: Dr. Schmeursh

Verdict: Very good Jardin de Ski, although it does get very overcrowded in the French holidays.

MONTGENÈVRE 1850m

GENERAL SKI INFORMATION
Top height: 2600m
Pistes (km): 60
Lifts: 34
Snow-making: Yes
Language: French

LIFT PASSES
Local pass covers Montgenèvre lifts only. Free pass up to age of 5.
Adult 6-day pass 540FF
6 days under 12s 415FF

SKI SCHOOL
E.S.F. SKI SCHOOL – 92 21 90 46

E.S.F. SKI SCHOOL
Age: 5 years and over
Days: Mon to Fri
Hours: 9.15am to 11.15am and 2.30pm to 5pm
English speaking instructors: 44%
Maximum in class: 12
Indoor recreation if weather bad: No
Supervised lunch: No
Prices: 91/92 prices 6-half-days – 430FF

KINDERGARTEN SKI SCHOOL
Age: 3 to 5 years
Days: Mon to Sat
Hours: 9am to 12noon and 2pm to 5pm
English speaking instructors: 50%
Supervised lunch: No
Ratio of children to instructor: 10:1
Location: Town centre
Indoor recreation if weather bad: Yes
Prices: 143FF per day, 6 days 682FF.

NURSERY
Age: 1 to 4 years
Days: Daily
Hours: 9am to 5.30pm
English speaking guardian: Yes
Facilities to play outside: Yes
Supervised lunch: No
Location: In the Tourist Office in town centre
Prices: 77FF per day, 6 days 440FF

BABYSITTING
General babysitting: List available from the Tourist Office
Hotels with nursery facilities: No

NON-SKIING ACTIVITIES
Indoor library and cinema, outdoor skating rink, curling, hang-gliding, paragliding, snow scooters.

CLOSEST AIRPORT
Turin – 2 ½ hours
Grenoble – 3 hours
Lyon – 4 hours

TOUR OPERATORS
Enterprise, Made to Measure, Thomson.

IMPORTANT TELEPHONE NUMBERS
Tourist Office: 92 21 90 22
Fax: 92 21 92 45
Doctor: Dr. Miro – 92 21 94 19

Verdict: Easy access to nursery slopes. Heavy traffic in main street.

GENERAL SKI INFORMATION
Top height: 2000m
Pistes (km): 650
Lifts: 230 (Portes du Soleil)
Snow-making: Yes
Language: French

LIFT PASSES
Adult 6-day pass 805FF
Under 12s 6-day pass 531FF
Free pass up to age of 4 years

E.S.F. SKI SCHOOL
Tel: 50 79 13 13
Age: 4 years and over
Days: Sun to Fri
Hours: 9am to 12 noon and 2pm to 5pm
English speaking instructors: 40%
Maximum in class: 12
Indoor recreation if weather bad: No
Supervised lunch: No
Prices: 6 days 650FF

KINDERGARTEN SKI SCHOOL
L'Outa – 50 79 26 00. Run in conjunction with the E.S.F. Ski school, children are taken for skiing lessons and taken back to L'Outa afterwards.
Age: 4 to12 years
Days: Sun to Fri
Hours: 8.30am to 6pm
English speaking instructors: 20%
Supervised lunch: Yes
Ratio of children to instructor: 12:1
Location: Town Centre
Indoor recreation: Yes
Prices: 977FF per week, lunch 30FF per day.

NURSERY
L'Outa – 50 79 26 00
Age: 2 months to 4 years
Days: Sun to Fri
Hours: 8.30am to 6pm
English speaking guardian: Yes
Facilities to play outside: Yes
Supervised lunch: Yes
Location: Town centre
Prices: 173FF per day, 6 days 815FF, lunch 30FF per day extra.
NB A health certificate is required for children under 18 months.

BABYSITTING
General babysitting: List available from Tourist Office
Prices: Approx 40FF per hour
Hotels with nursery facilities:
Hotel le Petit Dru – 50 79 00 42, own crèche from 3 months to 10 years. 9am to 5pm. Residents only. No charge.
Hotel Regina – 50 79 20 66 – Tel. for info, unknown at time of going to print.

NON-SKIING ACTIVITIES
Indoor skating, curling, bowling, cinemas, sauna, massage, gym, table tennis, outdoor horse-riding, sleigh rides, paragliding.

CLOSEST AIRPORT
Geneva – 2 hrs

TOUR OPERATORS
Chalets and Hotels "Unlimited", Crystal, Enterprise, Made to Measure, Neilson, Ski Esprit.

IMPORTANT TELEPHONE NUMBERS
Tourist Office: 50 79 03 45
Fax: 50 79 03 48
Doctor: Dr Julien – 50 79 08 62

Verdict: Very good family resort. Morzine is an old French town with plenty of chalet accommodation.

LA PLAGNE 1800m

GENERAL SKI INFORMATION
Top height: 3250m
Pistes (km): 205
Lifts: 111
Snow-making: Yes
Language: French
Ski Club rep

LIFT PASSES
Covers all lifts in La Plagne and ski bus.
Adult 6-day pass 875FF.
Under 13s 6-day pass 660FF.
Free pass up to age of 6 years.

SKI SCHOOLS
E.S.F. Plagne Centre – 79 09 00 41
E.S.F. Plagne Village – 79 09 04 40
E.S.F. Plagne 1800 – 79 09 09 64
E.S.F. Plagne Soleil – 79 09 20 95
E.S.F. Plagne Bellecote – 79 09 05 91
E.S.F. Belle Plagne – 79 09 06 68
E.S.F. Aime La Plagne – 79 09 04 75

E.S.F. SKI SCHOOL – Plagne Centre
Age: 5 years and over
Days: Sun to Fri
Hours: 4 hours per day
English speaking instructors: 90%
Maximum in class: Approx 10
Indoor recreation if weather bad: No
Supervised lunch: Yes
Prices: 6 days with ski pass 750FF

KINDERGARTEN SKI SCHOOL
Age: 3 to 5 years (may vary slightly depending on Ski school).
Days: Sun to Fri
Hours: 4 hours a day
English speaking instructors:90%
Supervised lunch: Yes
Ratio of children to instructor: 10:1
Location: All fairly central
Indoor recreation if weather bad: Yes
Prices: 6 days – 570FF, mornings 85FF
NB Most of the E.S.F. ski schools run kindergartens in conjunction with ski tuition.

NURSERY
Age: 18 months to 4 years (depends on centre)
Days: Sun to Fri
Hours: 9am to 12 noon and 2pm to 5pm
English speaking guardian: Yes
Facilities to play outside: Yes
Supervised lunch: Yes
Location: Plagne Centre, Belle Plagne
Prices: One day 78FF

General babysitting: List available from the Tourist Office
Price: Approx 40FF per hour
Hotels with nursery facilities:
Club Aquarius – 79 09 10 10
Club Med – 79 22 24 26

NON-SKIING ACTIVITIES
Swimming pools, saunas, solariums, skating, squash, fitness centre, cinemas, bob-sleigh, paraskiing, skidoos, hang-gliding, outdoor skating rink.

CLOSEST AIRPORT
Geneva – 3 ½ hours

TOUR OPERATORS
Chalets and Hotels "Unlimited" Club Med, Crystal, Enterprise, Inghams, Made to Measure, Neilson, Total Ski, Thomson.

IMPORTANT TELEPHONE NUMBERS
Tourist Office: 79 09 02 01
Fax: 79 09 27 00
Doctor: Medical Clinic – 79 09 04 66

Verdict: Traffic free, purpose built resort. Good kindergarten ski schools and children's facilities.

GENERAL SKI INFORMATION
Top height: 3439m
Pistes (km): 300
Lifts: 120
Snow-making: Yes
Language: French
Ski Club rep

LIFT PASSES
Adult 6-day pass 870FF.
5 to 13 year old 6-day pass 615FF.
Free pass up to age of 5 years.

SKI SCHOOL
E.S.F. – 79 06 30 28
Evolution 2 (Val Claret) – 79 06 43 78

E.S.F. SKI SCHOOL
Age: 4 years and over
Days: Sun or Mon for 5 days
Hours: 9am to 12 noon – 2pm to 5pm
English speaking instructors: 80%
Maximum in class: 10
Indoor recreation: No
Supervised lunch: Yes
Prices: 5 days 770FF

KINDERGARTEN SKI SCHOOL
Les Marmottons – Tel 79 06 51 67
or 79 06 51 67
Age: 2 ½ to 12 years
Days: Daily
Hours: 8.45am to 5pm
English speaking instructors: 100%
Supervised lunch: Yes
Ratio of children to instructor: 10:1
Location: Tignes centre
Indoor recreation: Yes
Prices: 6 days with lunch 1150FF

Les Petits Lutens – 79 06 51 27
Age: 3 to 10 years
Days: Daily
Hours: 9am to 5pm
English speaking instructors: 100%

Supervised lunch: Yes
Ratio of children to instructor: 10:1
Indoor recreation if weather bad: Yes
Prices: 1250FF with lunch
NURSERY
Les Petits Lutens – 79 06 51 27
Age: 3 months to 3 years
Days: Daily
Hours: 8.30am to 5pm
English speaking guardian: Not guaranteed
Facilities to play outside: Yes
Supervised lunch: Yes
Location: 5 mins from town centre
Prices: 1250FF

BABYSITTING
General babysitting: A list is available from the Tourist Office
Prices: Approx 30FF per hour
Hotels with nursery facilities: No

NON-SKIING ACTIVITIES
Fitness club featuring weight training, aerobics, squash, golf practice, sauna, cinema, tennis, bowling, outdoor ice-rink, hang-gliding, deltaplanes, paragliding, helicopter rides, snow scooters, husky-drawn sleigh rides.

CLOSEST AIRPORT
Geneva – 4 ½ hours

TOUR OPERATORS
Bladon Lines, Chalets and Hotels "Unlimited", Club Med, Crystal, Enterprise, Inghams, , Made to Measure, Neilson, Ski Club of Great Britain, Supertravel, Thomson.

IMPORTANT TELEPHONE NUMBERS
Tourist Office: 79 06 15 55
Fax: 79 06 45 44
Doctor: Medical Centre – 79 06 50 07

Verdict: Although it has facilities for young children it can be very bleak and cold.

Val d'Isère 1850m

General ski information
Top height: 3439m
Pistes (km): 300
Lifts: 120
Snow-making: Yes
Language: French
Ski Club rep

Lift passes
Covers Val d'Isere, Tignes and buses.
Adult 6-day pass 870FF..
5 to 12 years 6-day pass 615FF
Free pass up to age of 5 years.

Ski schools
E.S.F. Ski School – 79 06 02 34
Snow Fun – 79 06 16 79 or 79 06 19 79
Evolution 2 – 79 41 16 72
Top Ski – 79 06 14 80

E.S.F. kindergarten ski school
Age: 4 years and over
Days: Sun to Fri
Hours: 9am to 12noon 2.30pm to 5pm
English speaking instructors: 100%
Maximum in class: 12
Indoor recreation if weather bad: No
Supervised lunch: Yes in school holidays
Prices: 6 days 950FF
NB The E.S.F. Ski school runs several courses for children depending on age and ability, but it should be noted that some of these are only available during the French school holidays.

Snow Fun
Nounours Club – 3 to 6 years, small classes. Sun to Fri $1\frac{1}{2}$hr, 2hr or 3 hr sessions. Children's ski school 4 to 13 years. Ski hire. 6 days with meals 1350FF.

Top Ski
Specialised teaching method for 3 year olds, pm only. Different classes for 5 years and over. All day small classes.

Evolution 2
5 to 7 years. Weekly classes with lunch.

Nursery
Le Petit Poucet – 79 06 13 97
Age: 3 to 8 years
Days: Daily
Hours: 9am to 5.30pm
English speaking guardian: Not guaranteed
Facilities to play outside: Yes
Supervised lunch: Yes
Location: 150m from town centre (free shuttle bus).
Prices: Approx 210FF per day with lunch and snacks.

NB Le Petit Poucet can arrange ski tuition in conjunction with the E.S.F. Ski school with transportation to and from the nursery to ski school with hours to suit age and ability of the child. Transport can also be arranged for collection of children before 9am and dropping off after 5.30pm.

Garderie Isabelle – 79 41 12 82
Les Tufs
Age: 2 years and over
Days: Daily
Hours: 8.30am to 5.30pm
English speaking guardian: Not guaranteed

Facilities to play outside:
Children taken for walks
Supervised lunch: Yes
Location: La Daille
Prices: 210FF per day with lunch
and snacks
Bout de Chou – 79 06 13 08
Mainly for Val d'Isere residents but
limited space for visitors.
Babies from 3 months to 2 years.
Open 8am to 6pm, but children are
only allowed to stay for a maximum
of 8 hours per day. 200FF per day
includes lunch and nappies etc.
Advance reservation essential.

BABYSITTING
General babysitting: A list of
babysitters is available from the
Tourist Office
Prices: Approx 40FF to 50FF per
hour
Hotels with nursery facilities: No

NON-SKIING ACTIVITIES
Swimming pool, fitness club featuring sauna, weight training, aerobics,
solarium, gym, cinema, outdoor skating rink, curling, hang-gliding, motor
trikes, snowmobile rides, paragliding.

CLOSEST AIRPORT
Geneva – $4\frac{1}{2}$ hours

TOUR OPERATORS
Bladon Lines, Chalets and Hotels
"Unlimited", Club Med, Crystal,
Enterprise, Inghams, Made to
Measure, Mark Warner, Neilson,
Supertravel, Thomson.

IMPORTANT TELEPHONE NUMBERS
Tourist Office: 79 06 10 83
Fax: 79 06 04 56
Doctor: Dr. Harris – 79 06 13 70

Verdict: One of the world's great resorts with plenty of skiing for young children.

Valmorel 1400m

General ski information

Top height: 2550m
Pistes (km): 163
Lifts: 47
Snow-making: Yes
Language: French

Lift passes

Adult 6-day pass 793FF
Under 13s 6-day pass 678FF
Free pass up to the age of 4 years

Ski school

E.S.F. Ski School – 79 09 81 86

Ski school

Age: 4 year upwards
Days: Mon to Sat
Hours: 9.30am to 12 noon and 2pm to 4.30pm
English speaking instructors: 80%
Maximum in class: 12
Indoor recreation if weather bad: No
Supervised lunch: No
Prices: 6days 450FF or 1159FF with lift pass

Kindergarten ski school

The Children's Village
Age: From 3 years upwards
Days: Sun to Fri
Hours: 8.30am to 12 noon and 1.30pm to 5.pm
English speaking instructors: 100%
Supervised lunch: Yes
Ratio of children to one instructor: 10:1
Location: Town centre
Indoor recreation if weather bad: Yes
Prices: 6 days 790FF plus 331FF for lunch, half-day 98FF.

Nursery

Saperlipopette, The Children's Village – 79 09 85 55
Age: 6 months to 8 years
Days: Sun to Fri
Hours: 8.30am to 5pm
English speaking guardian: Yes
Facilities to play outside: Yes
Supervised lunch: Yes
Location: Town centre
Prices: 6 days 790FF. Lunch 6 days 331FF
NB The Club's large building contains playrooms, a dining room, rest rooms and sunny terrace.

Babies from 6-18 months are looked after by qualified staff in the nursery which has a specially adapted kitchen for feeding bottles and baby food.

Toddlers from 18 months to 3 years have a special play area in the snow garden in addition to their indoor playrooms and rest rooms.

Children from 3 to 8 years can learn to ski on the Club's specially adapted slopes. After-skiing activities include the library, video room, cartoons, painting and handiwork.

It is advisable to book up for the Saperlipopette well in advance as it is very popular.

Babysitting

General babysitting: A list is available from the Tourist Office.
Prices: Approx 30FF to 40FF per hour.
Hotels with nursery facilities: No

NON-SKIING ACTIVITIES
Fitness club, sauna, gym, cinema,
tobogganing, floodlit skiing, snow-
shoe outings.

CLOSEST AIRPORT
Geneva – 4 hrs
Lyon – 3 ½ hrs

TOUR OPERATORS
Crystal, Enterprise, Inghams, Made
to Measure, Neilson, Simply Ski,
Thomson.

IMPORTANT TELEPHONE NUMBERS
Tourist Office: 79 09 85 55
Fax: 79 09 85 29
Doctor: Medical clinic – 79 09 80 45

Verdict: An excellent resort for children. The Children's Village must be pre-booked.

VAL THORENS 2300m

GENERAL SKI INFORMATION
Top height: 3400m
Pistes (km): 600 (Trois Vallees)
Lifts: 190
Snow-making: Yes
Language: French
Ski Club rep

LIFT PASSES
Adult 6-day pass 960FF (Trois Vallees)
5 to 16 years 6-day pass 720FF (Trois Valless)
Free pass up to the age of 5 years

SKI SCHOOL AND KINDERGARTEN
E.S.F. Ski School – 79 00 04 44
Age: 3 to 12 years
Days: Sun to Fri
Hours: 9am to 12.15pm and 2.45pm to 4.45pm (times will vary)
English speaking instructors: 100%
Maximum in class: 14
Indoor recreation if weather bad: Yes
Supervised lunch: Yes
Prices: Etoile Course, all day with lunch from Sun pm 1180FF.
Half-day group, 3 hrs a day from Mon to Fri – 460FF.
Morning and afternoon group, 3 hrs in the am and 2 hrs in the pm. Begins Sun pm but does not operate in the Christmas or February holidays 650FF.
Junior Course, for children who have passed their third star. Only available in February, from Sun pm to Fri, 3hrs in the am and 2 in the pm. Tests inc. 720FF.
Competition Course, Mon to Fri 1100FF.

NURSERY 2 ESF **Mini-Clubs**
Age: 3 months to 3 years

Days: Sun to Fri
Hours: 9.15am to 12.15pm and 2.15pm to 5.15pm
English speaking guardian: Yes
Facilities to play outside: Yes
Supervised lunch: Yes
Location: One Mini-Club in Les Temples du Soleil – 79 00 03 09
One Mini-Club in Roc de Peclat – 79 00 06 74
Prices: 6 days with lunch 1000FF, 6 half-days without a meal 460FF.
Reservations are essential

Marielle Goitchels children's village:
Ex-racer runs a ski kindergarten and holidays for children.

BABYSITTING
General babysitting: Ask at the Tourist Office.
Prices: Approx 50FF per hour
Hotels with nursery facilities: No

NON-SKIING ACTIVITIES
Club Pierre Barthes with swimming pool, sauna, fitness, jacuzzi, tennis school, squash and golf practice. snow bikes, hang-gliding, cinema.

Closest airport
Chambery – 2hrs
Geneva – 4 hrs

TOUR OPERATORS
Crystal, Enterprise, Inghams, Made to Measure, Neilson, Ski club of GB, Thomson.

IMPORTANT TELEPHONE NUMBERS
Tourist Office: 79 00 08 08
Fax: 79 00 00 04
Doctor: Medical Centre 79 00 00 37

Verdict: Good resort for late season holidays. Can be very cold and bleak in early season.

Switzerland

AROSA 1775m

GENERAL SKI INFORMATION
Top height: 2653m
Pistes (km): 70
Lifts: 17
Snow-making: No
Language: German
Ski Club rep

LIFT PASSES
Adult 6-day pass 197SF
Under 16s 6-day pass 99SF
Free up to the age of 6 years

SKI SCHOOL
Swiss Ski school – 81 31 1996

SWISS SKI SCHOOL
Age: 4 years
Days: Mon to Fri
Hours: 9.45am to 11.45am and
2.15pm to 4.15pm
English speaking instructors:
80%
Maximum in class: 15
Indoor recreation if weather
bad: No
Supervised lunch: No
Prices: 5 days 155SF
Ski races are organised every
Thursday.

KINDERGARTEN SKI SCHOOL
Age 4 years
Days: Mon to Fri
Hours: 9.45am to 11.45am and
2.15pm to 4.15pm
English speaking instructors:
80%
Supervised lunch: No
Ratio of children to instructor: 15:1
Location: 10 minutes by bus
Indoor recreation if weather
bad: No

Prices: 5 days 155SF

NURSERY – No

BABYSITTING
General babysitting: A list is available from the Tourist Office
Prices: Approx 15/20SF per hour
Hotels with nursery facilities:
Hotel Eden – 81 31 02 61, Hotel Park
– 81 31 01 65, Hotel Hof Maran – 81
31 01 85. All these hotels have supervised nurseries.

NON-SKIING ACTIVITIES
Indoor swimming pools in hotels, ice-skating, curling, sleigh-rides, indoor swimming pools in hotels, horse-riding, tobogganing, snow-shoe walks.

CLOSEST AIRPORT
Zurich – 2 ½ hours by train. No buses from airport.

TOUR OPERATORS
Swiss-ski, Made to Measure, Powder Byrne, Ski Club of Great Britain.

IMPORTANT TELEPHONE NUMBERS
Tourist Office: 81 31 1621
Fax: 81 31 3135
Doctor: Dr. Roethlisberger – 8131 1464

Verdict: Good family resort with excellent children's ski school. Lots to do after skiing.

GENERAL SKI INFORMATION
Top height: 3000m
Pistes (km): 160
Lifts: 42
Snow-making: Yes
Language: French
Ski Club rep

LIFT PASSES
Adult 6-day pass 201SF
Under 16s 6-day pass 120SF
Free pass up to the age of 6 years,
30% discount for families of three or
more.

SKI SCHOOL
Swiss Ski School
Crans – 27 41 13 20
Montana – 27 41 14 80

SKI SCHOOLS – Both
Age: 6 to 12 years
Days: Mon to Fri (6 half-days inc. all
day Thursday. Lunch on mountain).
Hours: 9.30am to 12.30pm
English speaking instructors: 50%
Maximum in class: 12
**Indoor recreation if weather
bad:** Yes
Supervised lunch: Yes
Price: 150SF (not inc lunch).

KINDERGARTEN SKI SCHOOL
Crans – 27 41 13 20
Age: 3 to 6 years
Days: Daily
Hours: 9.30am to 4pm
English speaking instructors:
50%
Supervised lunch: Yes
Ratio of children to instructor: 5:1
Location: Ski school meeting place
3/5 mins from town centre

**Indoor recreation if weather
bad:** Yes
Price: 5 days 150SF or 65SF per day
Montana – 27 41 14 80
Information same as Crans.
Location: Children's Ski school
meeting place – 5 mins
Price: 60SF per day
Price includes a hot or cold drink,
biscuit or chocolate, ski-test or bibi-
test.

NURSERY
Bibiland – 27 41 81 42
Age: 2 to 10 years
Days: Mon to Sat
Hours: 9am to 11.30am , 2pm to
6.30pm or all day.
English speaking guardian: Yes
Facilities to play outside: Yes
Supervised lunch: Yes
Location: Above Crans Tourist
Office
Price: am 12SF, pm 15F
All day 23SF inc. lunch.

Les Coccinelles
Montana – 27 41 47 98
Age: 18 months to 4 yrs
Days: Daily
Hours: 9am to 6pm
English speaking instructors:
Yes
Supervised lunch: Yes
Location: 5 mins from centre of
town
Prices: Half-day 22SF
Full day (inc lunch) 52SF
Age: 4 to 6 years
Info as above.
Prices: (To inc. morning ski lessons,
ski pass, lunch and ice-skating pass).
Half-day 37SF.

One day 70SF. One week 455SF
Les Coccinelles also takes boarders
and include special ski packages
escorted from London.

Fleur des Champs
Montana – 27 41 23 67
Age: 2 months to 12 years
Days: Daily
Hours: 8am to 6pm
English speaking instructors:
Very little although they do take
many English babies and toddlers.
Supervised lunch: Yes
Location: Between Crans and
Montana (short bus trip).

BABYSITTING
General babysitting: Ask at the
Tourist Office
Price: Negotiable
Hotels with nursery facilities: No

NON-SKIING ACTIVITIES
Tobogganing, indoor hotel swimming
pools open to the public, bowling,
squash, ice-skating, husky sled-rides
and curling.

CLOSEST AIRPORT
Geneva – $2\frac{1}{2}$ / 3 hours

TOUR OPERATORS
Swiss Ski, Bladon Lines, Inghams,
Made-to-Measure.

IMPORTANT TELEPHONE NUMBERS
Tourist Office: 27 41 21 32
Fax: 27 41 17 94
Doctor: Dr Guggi – 27 41 29 50

Verdict: Wide open sunny nursery slopes in Crans and
a good ski kindergarten make it worth a visit.

GENERAL SKI INFORMATION
Top height: 3018m
Pistes (km): 220
Lifts: 32
Snow-making: No
Language: German

LIFT PASSES
Adult 6-day pass 246SF
Under 16s 6-day pass 123SF
Free up to the age of 6 years

SWISS SKI SCHOOL
Tel: 81 39 14 38
Age: 6 to 12 years
Days: Mon to Fri
Hours: 9.30am to 11.30am and
1.30pm to 3.30pm
English speaking instructors: 80%
Maximum in class: 12
Indoor recreation if weather bad: No
Supervised lunch: Yes (parents provide packed lunch).
Prices: 5 days – 145SF (includes lunch supervision).
Children's races are held every Thursday with each participant receiving a souvenir medal.

KINDERGARTEN SKI SCHOOL
Age: 4 years
Days: Mon to Fri
Hours: 9.30am to 11.30am and
1.30pm to 3.30pm. Children in the ski kindergarten are looked after free of charge from 9am to 9.30am, 11.30am to 1.30pm and 3.30pm to 5pm. Free drink given.
English speaking instructors: 80%
Supervised lunch: Yes (parents provide packed lunch).
Ratio of children to instructor: 10:1

Location: 10 minutes from centre of town, access by free bus or T-bar ski lift.
Indoor recreation if weather bad: Yes
Price: Approx 145SF

NURSERY – No

BABYSITTING
General babysitting: List is available at Tourist Office
Prices: Approx 12/15SF per hour
Hotels with nursery facilities:
Park Hotel Waldhaus – 8139 01 81.
The supervised nursery is open to residents only, from 10am to 12noon and 2pm to 5pm for children from 2 years upwards. Extra babysitting is 20SF per hour. Children can be served supper from 5.30pm to 7pm.

NON-SKIING ACTIVITIES
Ice-skating, tobogganing, 5 hotel indoor swimming pools open to the public, bowling, horse drawn sleigh rides, curling. Prau la Selva sports centre offers fitness room and indoor shooting range. 2 indoor tennis courts at Park Hotel Waldhaus and paragliding.

CLOSEST AIRPORT
Zurich – 2 hours by coach

TOUR OPERATORS
Swiss Ski, Powder Byrne, Made to Measure.

IMPORTANT TELEPHONE NUMBERS
Tourist Office: 81 39 10 22
Fax: 81 39 43 08
Doctor: Dr Berthold – 81 39 13 13

Verdict: The ski school will look after children before and after classes at no extra cost.

GRINDELWALD 1040m

GENERAL SKI INFORMATION
Top height: 2971m
Pistes (km): 200
Lifts: 43
Snow-making: Yes
Language: German
Ski Club rep

LIFT PASSES
Adult 6-day pass 210SF
Under 16s 6-day pass 105SF
Free pass up to the age of 6 years if accompanied by an adult.

SWISS SKI SCHOOL
Tel: 36 53 20 21
Age: 3 to 14 years
Days: Mon to Fri
Hours: 10am to 12 noon and 2pm to 4pm
English speaking instructors: 90%
Maximum in class: 12
Indoor recreation if weather bad: No
Supervised lunch: Yes (at the Children's Club Bodmi).
Prices: 5 days 170SF
Thursday Children's ski race, Friday Prizegiving at 11.30am, Friday pm children's ski test.

Children's Club Bodmi
Tel: 36 53 20 21
Run by the ski school but no ski instruction given
Age: 3 years and over
Days: Mon to Fri
Hours: See price
Facilities to play outside: Yes
English speaking guardian: Yes
Location: 5 minutes with the Funicular which is free or a 15 minute walk, or it can be arranged to leave and collect your children from the ski school.
Price: Morning 9am to 12 noon SF10.
Afternoon with lunch, 12 noon to 4pm SF15.
Afternoon (excluding lunch) 2pm to 4pm SF10.
All day with lunch, 9am to 4pm SF35.

BABYSITTING
General babysitting: Ask at the Tourist Office.
Hotels with nursery facilities: 3 star – Sans Souci Hotel has an unsupervised playroom for children age 5 years and over.

NON-SKIING ACTIVITIES
Horse drawn sleigh rides, ice-skating, tobogganing, paragliding, Sports Centre offering swimming, sauna, solarium, table tennis, curling and indoor ice-skating.
The World Snow festival takes place from January 24th to 30th each year featuring teams from all over the world who create wonderful ice sculptures.

CLOSEST AIRPORT
Zurich – 2hrs
Geneva – 3hrs

TOUR OPERATORS
Inghams, Supertravel, Made to Measure, Powder Byrne.

IMPORTANT TELEPHONE NUMBERS
Tourist Office: 36 53 12 12
Fax: 36 53 30 88
Doctor: Dr. Strupler – 36 53 45 45

Verdict: Highly recommended for families.

GENERAL SKI INFORMATION
Top height: 2865m
Pistes (km): 155
Lifts: 36
Snow-making: Yes
Language: Swiss German

LIFT PASSES
Covers lifts in Lenzerheide, Valbella, Parpan and Churwalden and bus.
Adult 6 day pass 197SF
Under 16s 6 day pass 118SF
Free pass up to the age of 6 years

SWISS SKI SCHOOL
Tel: 81 34 19 33
Age: 5 years and over
Days: Mon to Fri
Hours: 10am to 3pm (with one hour lunch)
English speaking instructors: 85%
Maximum in class: 20 (school hols)
Indoor recreation if weather bad: No
Supervised lunch: Yes
Prices: 5 days185SF – 5 half-days 126SF

KINDERGARTEN SKI SCHOOL
Age: 4 years and over
Days: Mon to Fri
Hours: 10am to 12 noon
English speaking instructors: 85%
Supervised lunch: No
Ratio of children to instructor: 10:1
Location: Town centre
Indoor recreation if weather bad: No
Prices: 5 mornings 126SF

NURSERY
Hotel Schweizerhof – 81 34 01 11
Age: From birth.
Days: Mon to Fri
Hours: 9am to 7pm
English speaking guardian: Sometimes
Facilities to play outside: Yes
Supervised lunch: Yes
Location: Lenzerheide town centre
Prices: One day with lunch 15SF

NURSERY
Hotel Valbella – 81 34 36 36
Age: Any age
Days: Daily
Hours: 8am to 9pm
English speaking guardian: Yes
Facilities to play outside: Yes
Supervised lunch: Yes
Location: Valbella (3kms - free bus from Lenzerheide)
Price: Half-day 18SF, one day with lunch 36SF

BABYSITTING
General babysitting: A list is available from the Tourist Office
Prices: Negotiable
Hotels with nursery facilities:
Hotel Valbella – 81 34 36 36
Hotel Schweizerhof – 81 34 01 11

NON-SKIING ACTIVITIES
Sports centre with swimming, sauna, jacuzzi, solarium, curling, skating; fitness centre, cinema, tennis, squash, bowling, outdoor skating rink, toboggan runs, sleigh rides, ski bobs.

CLOSEST AIRPORT
Zurich - $2\frac{1}{2}$ hours

TOUR OPERATORS
Inghams, Made to Measure, Swiss-Ski

IMPORTANT TELEPHONE NUMBERS
Tourist Office: 81 34 34 34
Fax: 81 34 53 83
Doctor: Dr Durband – 81 34 12 30

Verdict: **Friendly Swiss village with good nursery slopes. Recommended.**

St Moritz 1800m

GENERAL SKI INFORMATION
Top height: 3300m
Pistes (km): 400
Lifts: 60
Snow-making: Yes
Language: German
Ski Club rep

LIFT PASSES
Adult 6-day pass 236SF
Free pass up to the age of 6 years

SKI SCHOOL
Swiss Ski School – 82 380 90
Suvretta Ski School – 82 344 90

SWISS SKI SCHOOL
Age: 4 years and over
Days: Sun to Fri
Hours: 10am to 12 noon and 1.30pm to 3.30pm
English speaking instructors: 60%
Maximum in class: 8
Indoor recreation if weather bad: Yes
Supervised lunch: Yes
Price: 6 days with lunch 350SF

KINDERGARTEN SKI SCHOOL
Age: 4 years and over
Days: Sun to Fri
Hours: 10am to 12 noon and 1.30pm to 3.30pm
English speaking instructors: 90%
Supervised lunch: Yes
Ratio of children to teacher: 5:1
Location: On the mountain but children are collected and delivered to the Ski School meeting places in Dorf and Bad.
Indoor recreation if weather bad: Yes
Prices: 6 days 350SF

NURSERY
Parkhotel Kurhaus
Age: 3 years and over
Days: Sun to Fri
Hours: 9am to 4.30pm
English speaking guardian: Yes
Supervised lunch: Yes
Ratio of children to guardian: Not known
Location: St Moritz Bad
Prices: 30SF per day with lunch

BABYSITTING
General babysitting: List available at the Tourist Office
Hotels with nursery facilities:
Hotel Carlton – 82 21 141
Hotel Schweizerhof – 82 22 171
Both these hotels have supervised kindergartens for 3 years and over. The Carlton is for residents only and the Schweizerhof will give priority to residents.

NON-SKIING ACTIVITIES
Ice-rink, sleigh-rides, swimming, curling, indoor tennis, squash, cinema, sauna/solarium, museum, hanggliding, golf on frozen lake.

CLOSEST AIRPORT
Zurich – 4 hrs by train

TOUR OPERATORS
Swiss Ski, Inghams, Thomson, Club Med, Made to Measure, Powder Byrne, Supertravel.

IMPORTANT TELEPHONE NUMBERS
Tourist Office: 82 33 147/48
Fax: 82 32 952
Doctor: Dr Gut – 82 34 141

Verdict: Quite a lot of walking involved and the bus is usually overcrowded.

GENERAL SKI INFORMATION
Top height: 2970m
Pistes (km): 50
Lifts: 8
Snow-making: Yes
Language: Swiss German
Ski Club rep

LIFT PASSES
Adult 6 day pass 210SF
Under 16s 6 day pass 105SF
Free ski pass up to age of 6 accompanied by an adult.

SKI SCHOOL
Swiss ski school - 36 55 12 47

SWISS SKI SCHOOL
Age: 4 years and over
Days: Mon to Sat
Hours: 10.00am to 12 noon
English speaking instructors: 90%
Maximum in class: 10
Indoor recreation if weather bad: Yes
Supervised lunch: No
Prices: Weekly card - 6 x 2 hour classes 102SF

KINDERGARTEN SKI SCHOOL - No

NURSERY
Tel: 36 55 12 47
Age: 2 to 6 years
Days: Mon to Sat
Hours: 9am to 12.15pm and 12.15pm to 4pm.
English speaking guardian: Yes
Facilities to play outside: Yes
Supervised lunch: Yes (children must take packed lunch).
Location: At the Sports Centre in town

Prices: 6 half-days 155SF, one day 20SF.

BABYSITTING
General babysitting: Contact the Fewo Service - 36 55 37 06
Hotels with nursery facilities: No

NON- SKIING ACTIVITIES
Tobogganing, ice-skating, curling, Alpine Sports Centre which includes swimming pool, children's pool, whirl-pool, library, children's playroom, gym, solarium, massage.

CLOSEST AIRPORT
Zurich - 3 ½ hrs

TOUR OPERATORS
Swiss-Ski, Made to Measure, Supertravel.

IMPORTANT TELEPHONE NUMBERS
Tourist Office: 36 55 16 16
Fax: 36 55 37 69
Doctor: Dr. Heimlinger – 36 55 17 10

Verdict: Attractive, peaceful, traffic-free village. Highly recommended for children who can ski.

SAAS-FEE 1800m

GENERAL SKI INFORMATION
Top height: 3500m
Pistes (km): 80
Snow making: Yes
Lifts: 26
Language: German

LIFT PASSES
Adult 6 day pass approx 210SF
Under 16s 6 day pass 140SF
Free pass up to age of 6 years

SKI SCHOOL
Swiss Ski School - 28 57 23 48

SKI SCHOOL
Age: 5 to 12 years
Days: Mon to Fri
Hours: 9.45am to 11.45 am and
1.30pm to 3.30pm
English speaking instructors: 100%
Maximum in class: 10
Indoor recreation if weather bad: No
Supervised lunch: Yes
Prices: 5 days 160SF plus 19SF per day for lunch and supervision.

KINDERGARTEN SKI SCHOOL/ NURSERY
At time of going to print the Tourist Office were unsure of what facilities would be available.

BABYSITTING
General babysitting: A list is available from the Tourist Office
Prices: Approx. 10-15SF per hour
Hotels with nursery facilities:
Hotel Alphubel - 28 57 11 12, has a nursery with two guardians from 8.00am to 6.00pm, for residents only, usually from 3 years but will try to accommodate younger children for shorter periods.

NON-SKIING ACTIVITIES
Bielen Leisure centre with swimming pool, jacuzzi, steam bath, solaria, sauna, tennis and gym and natural outdoor ice-rink with skating, curling, ice-hockey, ski-bob runs and toboggan run.

CLOSEST AIRPORT
Geneva - 3 hrs.

TOUR OPERATORS
Bladon Lines, Crystal, Enterprise, Inghams, Made to Measure, Supertravel, Swiss Ski, Swiss Travel,Thomson.

IMPORTANT TELEPHONE NUMBERS
Tourist Office: 28 57 14 57
Fax: 28 57 18 60
Doctor: Dr. Kuonen - 28 23 16 25

Verdict: Good nursery slopes for mid-season holidays. Very little for under 5s.

GENERAL SKI INFORMATION
Top height: 3328m
Pistes (km): 400
Snow-making: Yes
Lifts: 100 in 4 Valleys area
Language: French
Ski Club rep

LIFT PASSES
Adult 6 day pass (inc Mont Fort)
284SF.
Under 16s 6 day pass 142SF.
Free pass up to the age of 6 years.
Family ski pass - Father pays 100%,
mother 40% discount, children 16 to
20 years 40% discount and 3 to 16
years 70% discount.

SKI SCHOOL
Swiss Ski School - 26 31 68 25

SWISS SKI SCHOOL
Age: 3 to 12 years
Days: Sat to Sun
School hols - Sun to Sat
Hours: Sun 10.00am to 12.15am and
Mon to Sat 9.15am to 11.45pm and
2.10pm to 4.30pm.
English speaking instructors: 60%
Maximum in class: 12
**Indoor recreation if weather
bad:** No
Supervised lunch: Yes
Prices: 10 lessons (either am or pm)
195SF plus 22SF for lunch.
School hols offer all-day courses for
children 225SF.

KINDERGARTEN SKI SCHOOL
Swiss Ski School - Mini Champion
Club
Age: 3 to 10 years
Days: Mon to Sat

Hours: 8.30am to 5.00pm
English speaking instructors: 100%
Supervised lunch: Yes
Ratio of children to instructor: 10:1
Location: 500m from centre of town
Organised indoor recreation: Yes
Prices: One day 50SF, 3 days
140SF, 6 days 250SF with lunch.
Half-day possibility.

NURSERY
Chez les Schtroumpfs - 26 31 65 85
Age: 0 to 5 years
Days: Mon to Sun
Hours: Mon to Sat 8.30am to 5.30pm
Sun 9.30am to 5.30pm
Facilities to play outside: Yes
English speaking guardian: Yes
Supervised lunch: Yes. Lunch is
included, only small babies need to
take their own food.
Location: 150m from the Swiss Ski
School 5 minutes walk from town
centre.
Prices: One day with lunch 45SF,
half-day with lunch 35SF,
half-day without lunch 25SF, just
lunch 11.30am to 2.00pm 18SF.

BABYSITTING
General babysitting: A list is
available from the Tourist Office.
Prices: Approx 12SF to 15SF per
hour
Hotels with nursery facilities:
NB - Although the 3 star Hotel de
Verbier, run by Patrick Bruchez and
his English wife Lynne, does not
have specific nursery or babysitting
facilities, Lynne will gladly supply
cots, high chairs and toys and has a
TV lounge with English videos. With
advance notice she is very happy to

buy in nappies etc. for your arrival
and can help arrange babysitters
during the day or evening.
Children's meals can be served early
in the evening - 26 31 66 88.

NON-SKIING ACTIVITIES
2 indoor swimming pools, skating,
curling, squash, sauna, solarium,
jacuzzi, cinema, fitness centre, ski-
bob run, hang-gliding, toboggan run.

CLOSEST AIRPORT
Geneva - 2 ½ - 3 hrs

TOUR OPERATORS
Bladon Lines, Chalets and Hotels
"Unlimited", Crystal, Made to
Measure, Mark Warner, Neilson, Ski
Club of Great Britain, Ski Esprit,
Thomson.

IMPORTANT TELEPHONE NUMBERS
Tourist Office: 26 31 62 22
Fax: 26 31 32 72
Doctor: Medical Clinic – 26 31 66 77

Verdict: Village and skiing is spread out and buses tend to
be overcrowded. Limited nursery slopes.

GENERAL SKI INFORMATION
Top height: 2970m
Pistes (km): 120
Snow-making: No
Lifts: 45 in total (Villars and Les Diablerets)
Language: French
Ski Club rep

LIFT PASSES
Adult 6 day pass approx 160SF
Under 16s 6 day pass 114SF
Covers Villars and Les Diablerets lifts. Free pass up to the age of 6. Family rates available for 3 or more people.

SKI SCHOOL
Swiss Ski School - 25 35 22 10
Modern Ski School - 25 35 20 43

SWISS SKI SCHOOL
Age: 4 to 12 years
Days: Mon to Sat
Hours: Beginners - 9.45am to11.30am. Intermediate/advanced - 10.15am to 12 noon
For intermediate and advanced children, the meeting place for Ski School is Bretaye, the main ski area above Villars. Children needing to be accompanied to their classes must be at the Ski School office at 9.00am.
English speaking instructors: 90%
Maximum in class: 10
Indoor recreation if weather bad: No
Supervised lunch: No
Prices: 6 days ski school, including ski pass SF460

KINDERGARTEN SKI SCHOOL
Swiss Ski School
Age: 3 to 12 years
Days: Mon to Sat
Hours: 9.00am to 16.30pm
English speaking instructors: 90%
Ratio of children to instructor: 7:1
Supervised lunch: Yes
Indoor recreation if weather bad: Yes, ice skating and games.
Kindergarten location: Centre of town, behind the station.
Prices: 6 days 275SF (inc ski lessons, lift pass, lunch & drink, recreation).

The Swiss Ski School organise competitions, free of charge, every Saturday for weekly pupils.

MODERN SKI SCHOOL
Age: 3 to 12 years
Days: Mon to Sat
Hours: 10.30am to 12.00 noon
English speaking instructors: 95%
Maximum in class: 10
Indoor recreation if weather bad: No
Supervised lunch: No
Prices: Beginners 6 x 1 ½ hours lessons 85SF.
Lessons are held on the Ski School's own slope with lift in the centre of town.

NURSERY (AND SKI SCHOOL)
Pré Fleuri: 25 35 23 48
Age: 3 to 12 years
Days: Daily
Hours: 9.00am to 5.00pm
English speaking guardians: Yes
Ratio of children to guardian: 2:1
Facilities to play outside: Yes
Supervised lunch: Yes
Location: Chesieres-Villars (outside

Villars, but the Pré Fleuri bus will collect and deliver your children from Villars).
Prices: 6 days 445SF

NB The Pré Fleuri is a children's club which has its own ski slope and lift for beginners and young children. Skis, boots, mono-skis and ice skates are all available from Pré Fleuri and they even kit the children out in their uniform for easy identification on the slopes. With such a good ratio of children to guardians, the groups are kept very small and the children therefore benefit from individual attention. Pre Fleuri also takes boarders for the week, should you want the children to go on a ski holiday without you. It is advisable to book in advance as this club is extremely popular.

BABYSITTING
General babysitting: A list is available from the Tourist Office.
Prices: Approx 15-20SF per hour
Hotels with nursery facilities: None

NON-SKIING ACTIVITIES
Indoor tennis, skating, curling, swimming pool, bowling, fitness centre, squash and cinema and outdoor horse riding, ski bob runs and paragliding

CLOSEST AIRPORT
Geneva - 1 ½ hours

TOUR OPERATORS
Club Med, Crystal, Hoverspeed Ski-Drive, Inghams, Made to Measure, Neilsons, Ski Esprit, Swiss Ski.

IMPORTANT TELEPHONE NUMBERS
Tourist Office: 25 35 32 32
Fax: 25 35 27 94
Doctor: Dr. R. Carven - 25 35 33 21-2

Verdict: Highly recommended.

GENERAL SKI INFORMATION
Top height: 2971m
Pistes (km): 100 (195 in Jungfrau Region)
Lifts: 20 (43 in Jungfrau Region)
Snow-making: Yes
Language: Swiss German
Ski Club rep

LIFT PASSES
Adult 6 day pass 210SF
Under 16s 6 day pass 105SF
Children not in Ski School under 6
years of age, free if accompanied by
an adult. Beginners from 4 years
upwards in Ski School will be advised
by their ski instructor.

SKI SCHOOL
Swiss Ski School - 36 55 20 22

SWISS SKI SCHOOL
Age: 4 years and over
Days: Sun to Fri
Hours: 10.00am to 12.00 noon and
2.00pm to 4.00pm
English speaking instructors: 90%
Maximum in class: 14
Indoor recreation if weather bad: Yes
Supervised lunch: No
Prices: Weekly card 216SF

KINDERGARTEN SKI SCHOOL
Age: 3 to 7 years
Days: Mon to Sat
Hours: Mon to Fri 8.45am to
4.30pm/ Sat 8.45am to 12.30pm
English speaking instructors: 100%
Supervised lunch: Yes
Ratio of children to instructor: 12:1
Kindergarten location: Centre of
town in Sports Pavillion
Indoor recreation if weather bad: Yes
Prices: 25SF per day which includes

lunch. 5 days (Mon to Fri) 110SF.
Sat 4SF per hour
NB Children are given the option of
whether they want to ski or simply
play.

NURSERY - No

BABYSITTING
General babysitting: A list is
available from the Tourist Office.
Price: Approx 20SF per hour
Hotels with nursery facilities:
The 4 star Silberhorn Hotel - 36 56
51 31 has a children's room with
games and toys where children are
supervised and given lunch, this service is free for hotel guests and children are taken from 1 year upwards.
The 4 star Park Hotel Beausite - 36
56 51 61. Kindergarten open 8.00am
to 7.00pm from 3 years and over.
Limited space, priority given to hotel
guests. 15SF per half day. One day 25SF.

NON-SKIING ACTIVITIES
Skating, curling, toboggan run, ski
bob, swimming pool, bowling, sleigh
rides, paragliding.

CLOSEST AIRPORT
Zurich - 2 ½ hours

TOUR OPERATORS
Club Med, Crystal, Inghams, Made
to Measure, Ski Club of GB,
Supertravel, Swiss-Ski, Thomson

IMPORTANT TELEPHONE NUMBERS
Tourist Office: 36 55 14 14
Fax: 36 55 30 60
Doctor: Dr. U Allenspach – 36 55 15 03

Verdict: Wide open pistes.
Recommended for children who want to ski.

ZERMATT 1620m

GENERAL SKI INFORMATION
Top height: 3900m
Pistes (km): 150
Lifts: 37
Snow-making: Yes
Language: German
Ski Club Rep

LIFT PASSES
Adult 6 day pass 264SF
Under 15s 6 day pass 132SF
Free pass up to 6 years

SKI SCHOOL
Swiss Ski School - 28 67 54 44

SWISS SKI SCHOOL
Age: 6 years and over
Days: 6 days
Hours: 9.00am to 12 noon and 1.00pm to 4.00pm
English speaking instructors: 80%
Maximum in class: 12
Indoor recreation if weather bad: Yes
Supervised lunch: Yes
Prices: 6 days with lunch 225SF

KINDERGARTEN SKI SCHOOL
Age: 2 to 6 years of age
Days: 6 days
Hours: 10.30am to 3.30pm
English speaking instructors: 75%
Supervised lunch: Yes
Ratio of children to instructor: 12:1
Location: 5 minutes walk from town centre
Indoor recreation if weather bad: Yes
Prices: 6 days with lunch 225SF

NURSERY
There are 2 hotel nurseries:

Seiler's Nursery at the Hotel Nicoletta situated in the centre of town - 28 66 11 51
Age: 2 to 8 years
Days: Mon to Fri
Hours: 9.00am to 5.00pm
English speaking guardian: Yes
Facilities to play outside: Yes
Supervised lunch: Yes
Prices: For children of hotel guests:
Full day, 9.00am to 5.00pm, inc lunch 22 SF.
Half day, 9.00am to 1.00pm, inc lunch 18SF.
Half day, 1.00pm to 5.00pm, not inc lunch 14SF.
Prices: For children not staying at hotel:
Full day inc lunch 50 SF
Half day inc lunch 35SFSF
Half day not inc lunch 30SF
NB This nursery is in the basement of the hotel and therefore rather stuffy with limited natural light.

Kinderclub at Hotel La Ginabelle located 150m from the Sunnegga lift - 28 67 45 35
Age: 2 to 6 years
Days: Daily
Hours: 9.00am to 5.00pm
English speaking guardian: Yes
Facilities to play outside: Yes, weather permitting the children are given ski lessons close to the nursery or if not skiing are taken for a walk twice a day.
Supervised lunch: Yes
Prices: Free if you are resident in the hotel.
Non-residents: Full day inc lunch SF85.
Half day, 9.00am to 1.00pm, inc

lunch SF50.
Half day, 1.00pm to 5.00pm, not inc
lunch SF45.
NB This attractive nursery is situated on the ground floor of the hotel in
large, cheerful and airy rooms with a
small rest area with mattresses and
duvets.

BABYSITTING
Helen Jordon 28 67 20 96 (Looks
after very young babies).
General babysitting: Ask at the
Tourist Office
Hotels with nursery facilities:
Hotel La Ginabelle and Hotel
Nicoletta

NON-SKIING ACTIVITIES
Curling, bowling, ice-hockey, ice
skating, swimming, sauna, sleigh
rides, hang-gliding, fitness centre,
billiards.

CLOSEST AIRPORT
Geneva and Zurich - 4 to 5 hrs

TOUR OPERATORS
Bladon Lines, Chalets and Hotels
"Unlimited", Enterprise, Inghams,
Kuoni, Made to Measure, Mark
Warner, Neilsons, Powder Byrne,
Ski Club of Great Britain,
Supertravel, Swiss-Ski, Thomson.

IMPORTANT TELEPHONE NUMBERS
Tourist Office: 28 66 11 81
Fax: 28 66 11 85
Doctor: Dr. W. Schaller 28 67 30 20

Verdict: A lovely resort. Car-free, but quite a bit of
walking involved getting to the slopes.

Italy

GENERAL SKI INFORMATION
Top height: 3470m
Pistes (km): 100
Lifts: 26
Snow-making: Yes
Language: Italian

LIFT PASSES
No discount for children, but some lifts are free for beginners.
Prices: 6 days 2000,000 L

SKI SCHOOL
Monte Bianco - 165 84 24 77

SKI SCHOOL
Age: 4 years and over
Days: Sat or Sun for 6 days
Hours: 10am to 1pm
English speaking instructors: 20%
Maximum in class: 12
Indoor recreation if weather bad: No
Supervised lunch: No
Prices: 6 days 160,000 L

Kindergarten/nursery -
Tel: 165 84 50 73
Age: 6 months to 3 years
Days: Daily
Hours: 9am to 4pm
English speaking guardian: Yes
Facilities to play outside: Yes
Supervised lunch: Yes
Location: The Kinderheim del Plan Checrouit, situated at the top of the main cable-car.
Prices: Unknown at time of going to print.

BABYSITTING
General babysitting: List available at the Services Centre - 165 84 51 51

Prices: Negotiable.
Hotels with nursery facilities: No

NON-SKIING ACTIVITIES
Indoor swimming pool, ice-skating, walks, paragliding, tennis, museum, bridge.

CLOSEST AIRPORT
Geneva - 1 ½ hrs
Turin - 2hrs
Milan - 3 hrs

TOUR OPERATORS
Bladon Lines, Crystal, Enterprise, Inghams, Mark Warner, Neilson, Thomson.

IMPORTANT TELEPHONE NUMBERS
Tourist Office: 165 84 20 60
Fax: 165 84 20 72
Doctor: Dr. Rocchio - 165 84 11 13

Verdict: The kindergarten is at the top of the cable-car.

SAUZE D'OULX 1500m

GENERAL SKI INFORMATION
Top height: 2820m
Pistes (km): 100
Lifts: 28
Snow-making: Yes
Language: Italian

LIFT PASSES
Covers Sauze, Sansicario, Claviere, Cesana and Sestriere lifts (27 in total).
8 years to adult 6-day pass 200,000L.
Free pass up to age 8 if accompanied by an adult.

SKI SCHOOLS
Sauze Project - 122 85 89 42
Sauze Sportina - 122 85 02 18
Sauze D'Oulx - 122 85 80 84

SKI SCHOOL - All
Age: 4 years and over
Days: Sun to Sat or Mon to Sun
Hours: 10.00am to 1.00pm
English speaking instructors: 80%
Maximum in class: 11
Indoor recreation if weather bad: No
Supervised lunch: No
Prices: Not available at time of going to print but 1991/92 6 days approx 140,000L.

KINDERGARTEN SKI SCHOOL - No

NURSERY
Age: 6 months to 6 years
Days: Daily
Hours: 9.00am to 5.00pm
English speaking guardian: Yes
Facilities to play outside: Yes
Supervised lunch: Yes, but children must bring a packed lunch.
Location: 100m from town centre
Prices: Not available at time of going to print but 1991/92 6 half-days - 180,000L. 6 days 91/92 250,000L.

BABYSITTING
General babysitting: Tourist Office does not have a list but will try and help.
Prices: Approx LR11,000 per hour
Hotels with nursery facilities: Hotel Sportina (residents only and very isolated).

NON-SKIING ACTIVITIES
Indoor tennis, bowling, cinema, ice rink, swimming pool, sauna, gym, volleyball and squash. Outdoor skating rink, tobogganing, hang-gliding, parapenting.

CLOSEST AIRPORT
Turin - 2 hours

TOUR OPERATORS
Enterprise, Neilson, Ski Global, Thomson.

IMPORTANT TELEPHONE NUMBERS
Tourist Office: 122 85 497
Fax: 122 85 497
Doctor: Dr Prunelli - 122 83 26 02

Verdict: Not recommended for very young children because of the walking involved.